THE FOLKLORE AND FOLKLIFE SERIES
Kenneth S. Goldstein, General Editor

Henry Glassie
Pattern in the Material Folk Culture
of the Eastern United States

Alan Brody
The English Mummers and Their Plays

Pierre Maranda and Elli Maranda (eds.)
Structural Analysis of Oral Tradition

Samuel G. Armistead and Joseph H. Silverman (eds.)
Judeo-Spanish Ballads from Bosnia

John Fought
Chorti Mayan Texts

Roberta Reeder (ed.)
Down Along the Mother Volga

Barbara Kirshenblatt-Gimblett (ed.)
Speech Play
(also a volume in the Conduct and Communication Series)

The Life

The Life.

The Lore and Folk Poetry of the Black Hustler

DENNIS WEPMAN
RONALD B. NEWMAN
MURRAY B. BINDERMAN

University of Pennsylvania Press

1976

Acknowledgments

Some of the introductory material for this book has been presented in different form in the following places: at the 1974 meeting of the Eastern Sociological Society in Philadelphia; at the 1974 conference of the Popular Culture Association in Milwaukee; at the 1974 meeting of the American Sociological Association in Montreal; in the *Journal of American Folklore*; and in *Urban Life: A Journal of Ethnographic Research*.

For advice and help, we owe special thanks to Bruce Jackson, Michael Agar, Alan Dundes, Roger D. Abrahams, Seymour Fiddle, and Robert Erwin.

Contents

GLOSSARY AND BIBLIOGRAPHY

INDEX

Introduction

Out of the black urban experience have come many revealing expressions of a culture with distinct values and a style of its own. Perhaps none of these expressions is so vivid and illuminating as the folk poems known as *toasts*, thirty-four of which are offered here.

Toasts are a form of poetry recited by certain blacks—really a performance medium, widely known within a small (and probably disappearing) community and virtually unheard of outside it. They are like jokes: no one knows who creates them, and everyone has his own versions.

But toasts, like any other stylized form of expression, have their own conventions of form and content. Furthermore, they come from a clearly defined subculture and meet all the standard criteria of folk literature: dispersion and longevity as well as anonymity and mutability. Though some toasts are pure boast or precept, the most common type is narrative—stories ranging from simple anecdote to highly elaborated, almost epic tales.

In all these types, narrative and non-narrative, we see revealed, as no academic study reveals, the special community which creates and transmits toasts: that black urban subculture known as sporting life, or, simply, the Life. It is always risky to describe a sociological "community" as if it had precise boundaries; but in toasts we can see certain social roles and behavior patterns which sketch, at least in rough outline, something of a portrait of the community that generates these verses.

THE LIFE

The Life has been variously defined: the world of prostitution, the world of drug addiction, the entire "culture of poverty." But the Life is both more and less than these.

Not all urban, lower-class blacks, of course, participate in the Life, though many have daily contact with it; and such peripheral types as "street cats" and "shadies" are not members, though these groups frequently interact with those who truly belong to the Life. Whereas street cats and shadies operate in sometimes legal but always socially disapproved occupations connected with areas such as the liquor trade, those in the Life are engaged in unquestionably illegal activities.

People in the Life engage in petty crimes like shoplifting or in victimless crimes—those in which people's desires are exploited, in which the criminal is approached with a request to supply some non-lawful product or service: sex, narcotics, gambling. Those crimes are committed with at least the implicit knowledge and frequently the active complicity of law-enforcement officials. The community of the Life is, in large measure, defined by such illicit activities and by the unique behavioral and cultural patterns they generate.

The Life includes a number of vital behavior patterns. Probably its most salient forms of activity are comprehended in the term Game—a pattern of exploitative interaction, usually between a member of the Life (a "player" of the Game) and an outsider in search of illicit or socially reproved goods or services obtainable through contact with the Life. The Game combines the struggle for survival with the ethic of free-enterprise competition as the player manipulates people and circumstances to take his victim's money. A player is often involved in several forms of the Game at the same time, though his primary source of income usually comes from one in particular. Games in the Life range from such low-risk activities as pool hustling or craps to such dangerous but potentially lucrative ones as selling drugs.

The elements of a specific game include the player, the goods or services offered or promised, and, of course, the customer or victim. A game is played at its most cunning and efficient by having a third party engage the victim, obtain his money, and give it to the player. This pattern characterizes pimping, the favored game in the Life.

The pimp may control one or more women, for whose sexual services he solicits willing males. But the pimp most respected in the Life does not solicit for his women; he depends on them to initiate contact with customers and obtain payment. This skillful pimp, sometimes distinguished as a "mackman," provides his women with food, clothing, shelter, protection, bail bond, attorney fees, and pocket money and generally manages their personal and professional lives. The women constitute a player's "stable of lace," bound to him by many and varied ties that may include fear, love, sexual passion, a desire for status, and the need for security. Though the pimp may engage in sexual relations with his women, his attraction for them depends more upon an aura and mere promise of superhuman sexuality, upon the magnetism of his personality, and upon the acuity of his verbal skills. Players recruit women by means of highly elaborated techniques, including "sweet talk," exploitative language skills developed early in life at such places as poolhalls and street corners.

The verbal skills of a youth may attract the attention of an older player willing to serve as a mentor, much as the talent of an apprentice would attract any craftsman. The youth undergoes a training course in the mechanics of running games, all the while honing his verbal skills, as vividly described in Honky-Tonk Bud's reminiscence in "The Return of Honky-Tonk Bud." For the player, with increasing proficiency comes increasing independence—not only from his mentor but from all affective relationships. For the pimp such detachment is manifest in an icy demeanor toward his women. In keeping with his male egoism, he is the major disciplinarian and the total ruler of his stable.

The relationship between the pimp and his women is, at least from his standpoint, economic rather than romantic. The male sees the female as a mesmerized subject under the control of his charismatic personality. The player's conception of women is tartly summed up in "The Fall": " 'A bitch can't shit without a good man's wit' " (1. 233).

A whore rarely remains with the same pimp for her entire career. She might, for example, find another pimp's line more persuasive or another situation more attractive. Thus a pimp must maintain his entrepreneurial skills and verbal ingenuity at a constantly high level to keep his stable performing harmoniously and productively. In fact, success at any of the games of the Life comes only with relentlessly hard work:

> You know the price when you deal in vice,
> You know it's a steady grind.
>
> ("The Fall," 11. 109–110)

But the demands of the Life extend beyond diligence. The Life is a glorification of virility, masculinity, male assertiveness. The player maintains a flamboyant life style through cars, clothing, and jewelry—and of course women—as an indication of distinctiveness and opulence. The automobile, regarded as an expression of the masculine self, is perhaps the most envied status symbol in the Life. The preferred vehicle is a powerful, expensive machismo-machine decorated with flair to project the individuality of its owner. The affluent player traditionally drives a Cadillac, especially the customized Eldorado. Toasts are studded with references to this car.

Clothing is an even more important element, one of the crucial means by which the player's uniqueness can be expressed. His wardrobe is the visible indicator, both to his peers and to the world at large, of his success in the Life, his skill at playing the Game. Clothing also proclaims the player's taste and style, yielding personal satisfaction and professional advantages such as attracting new women to his stable.

"Discovered" by clothing designers and fashion consultants, the player's sartorial styles increasingly influence the fashions of the larger society. Such men's clothing styles as wide, floppy-brimmed hats, high-heeled shoes, leather vests, and male shoulderbags either originated with players or gained fashion acceptance after appearing in the Life.

Toasts are replete with voluptuous descriptions of clothing. Good-Doing Wheeler's attire, for example, is marvelously extravagant:

> He had handkerchieves of the finest weaves,
>   He had them made by hand;
> His fabulous sky was broke so fly
>   That the city had it banned.
>
> His shoes were neat, they couldn't be beat,
>   Yet he wore each pair but once.
> They looked like suede, and dig how they was made—
>   From the hair of virgin cunts.
>
> ("Good-Doing Wheeler," 11. 9–16)

A related aspect of this quest for status in the Life is revealed by the many references in toasts to prestigious clothing firms; "Mexicana Rose" names five within the first twenty-four lines. The last note of luxury in the player's attire is expensive jewelry, like the Pool-Shooting Monkey's "Elgin ticker with a solid gold band" and "egg-sized diamond" (11. 15–16).

In the conspicuousness of his consumption and the immediacy of his gratification, the player seems to caricature certain features of the average American. The general goals of the Life do not differ from some of those often found in mainstream America; displayable wealth, for instance, is an aspiration common to both. A pimp's dream of a "blue Eldorado trimmed in pure gold" ("Mexicana Rose," 1. 114) is an exaggeration of one of the most common dreams of the average American.

Nevertheless, the player's extravagant expenditures on cars, clothing, and jewelry reveal cultural values that contrast with traditional views. Conventional American society puts a premium on prudence, on saving money to buy a home and support a family. In the Life, on the other hand, a player rents one furnished place after another, and the only family he supports is a stable of whores.

As a matter of fact, the goals of the player and those of his prudent counterpart proceed from quite different assumptions. When the mainstream American lavishes his money on displayable acquisitions, it is on the assumption that the future is predictable, secure, and promising. But when the player does so, it is precisely because he assumes the future to be unpredictable, insecure, and threatening. Though the Life has its pleasures—the fun, the swagger, the savoring of occasional success, the "high life" as distinct from the "good life" of the respectable world—players recognize them to be transient. A certain fatalism underlies the short-term outlook characteristic of the Life. This outlook is found throughout black experience as a function of poverty and social impotence. Toasts indicate that a fall lies at the end of every good run of luck.

> You ain't no lame, you know the Game,
> They call it cop and blow.
>
> ("The Fall," 11. 221–222)

PERFORMANCE

"Toasts," as Bruce Jackson remarks, "can be told anywhere" (1974:2).* But they are usually collected in institutions. The circumstance of institutional confinement is a natural one for the recitation of toasts, and collectors find it easier to gain access to such a setting than to the poolrooms and "shooting galleries" where the verses are recited "outside."

The toasts in this collection are no exception. They were taken down in shorthand from spontaneous recitations during the 1950's and 60's by one of us, at that time an inmate in the prisons of New York—Sing Sing, Clinton, Attica, and Auburn—but that doesn't mean they represent a prison genre. Almost all are concerned with life outside of institutions.

*All the writings to which we refer in this book are listed by author and date in the Bibliography, beginning on p. 193.

Telling toasts, like telling jokes, is a social entertainment; and like jokes toasts may be known by everyone in the audience but can be recited well only by people with special talents. A good toast-teller is as much of a specialist as a good raconteur in any other genre, and as rare.

People learn toasts from hearing them recited a few times; the verses are almost never committed to paper. Like all orally transmitted material, the form and content may change with each telling until the piece takes on something of a communal character. Considerations of an Ur-text are gratuitous; total freedom to augment, shorten, adapt, and improvise is one of the defining features of a toast. One session of "The Signifying Monkey" heard at Sing Sing went on for over an hour, the first teller being interrupted by others who remembered or invented couplets as he progressed. There are virtually no limits to some toasts: "The Ball of the Freaks," for example, may be recited, as "Madamoiselle from Armentieres" may be sung, for as long as the patience, ingenuity, or stamina of the crowd lasts.

But most recitation sessions are somewhat more structured: a reciter performs to a silent, appreciative audience. Good tellers may be highly valued and much in demand, both in institutions and out; they are invited to parties as good pianists are for their talents and fed drinks or dope for their services. Outside recitations are like any other social performance; friends exchange them as they do jokes or gossip. A good teller is almost never interrupted; others may follow with their versions, but a performance may be spellbinding while it is going on. In prison, where these toasts wers heard, they were often recited from a cell to an attentive audience on the same cellblock gallery, no one daring to interrupt the performance for anything less important than to warn of the approach of a guard. When they were recited in the recreation yard, the speaker would stand against a wall until the crowd he attracted was broken up by a guard.

In Attica, Doe Eye, a young burglar from Harlem who provided some of the best of those collected here, could characterize the people of the toasts so exactly that, when he was speaking from his cell, one might have thought he had a group in there with him, the falsetto of his Duriella du Fontaine so convincing that it was hard to believe it issued from the same mouth as his Tough Tony in "Death Row." Some toasts include speech by four or five characters, and a good performer cannot only keep them all distinct but do them all convincingly. Such star turns were as rare as any other feats of recitation, however, and the good tellers were valued accordingly. Most recitations were performed as lifelessly and haltingly as most jokes.

A good reciter among those known to us usually had a sizable repertoire, though with age the stock seemed to diminish. It was the younger tellers who seemed to have the largest collections and the freshest memories. In Auburn, Duke could recite toasts all day, though not particularly well. A sailor apparently in his early twenties (though no one could ever tell), Duke claimed to come from nowhere at all; he had been everywhere and rejoiced in his rootlessness. The toasts he knew had come from streets and ships, poolhalls and bars, prisons and drug rehabilitation centers. He had heard them from old and young, junkie and safe-cracker (the opposite ends of the prestige scale in prison). He was himself outside of age, place, and status, a free-floater acceptable in all circles but a part of none.

Few of the reciters, good or bad, truly belonged to the Life. The troubadour is seldom one of the heroes of whom he sings. But they had all been in contact with it, on the fringes, envious or contemptuous, but deeply affected by it. The older ones deplored the decaying standards of the Life, as we can see in some of the dismay expressed in "The Fall" ("They're just ruining the name of a hell of a game"), and the younger ones already saw it as a passing thing, almost quaint, being supplanted by organized crime and black militancy as a source of role models. Already by the 60's the wellsprings of toasts were drying up, and the verses had begun to assume the character of ballads, treasured artifacts of a romanticized past.

The times, the places, and the performers of the toasts reproduced in this book are indicated below:

1953–54 Sing Sing Prison, Ossining, N.Y.
  Bob ("Ball of the Freaks"; "Bill and Lil")
  Eddie ("Mexicana Rose")
  Otto ("Death Row")

1954–56 Clinton Prison, Dannemora, N.Y.
  Jim ("Master of the Long-Shoe Game"; "King Heroin II")
  Steve ("Pimping Sam")
  Superjunkie ("Good-Doing Wheeler"; "Broadway Sam"; "The Junkie";
    "King Heroin")

1956–64 Attica Prison, Attica, N.Y.
  Doe Eye ("Signifying Monkey II"; "The Fall"; "One Thin Dime";
    "Duriella du Fontaine")
  Lou ("Signifying Monkey"; "The Letter"; "Answer to 'The Letter' ")
  Washington ("Pool-Shooting Monkey"; "Konky Mohair")

1964–67 Auburn Prison, Auburn, N.Y.
  Big Stick ("Stagger Lee")
  Boxcar ("Return of Honky-Tonk Bud"; "The Hustler")
  Duke ("Honky-Tonk Bud"; "Dumbo the Junkie"; "Sugar Hill"; "Bad
    Dan"; "Bad Man Dan"; "Bill Skinner"; "Do Your Crying")
  Pop ("Wise Egg"; "Sporting Life")
  Slim ("Kitty Barrett"; "Do You Know What It Means?")

The Genre

Beyond the criteria that define toasts are other considerations that characterize the genre in more detail: *prosody,
diction, dramatic perspective, tone, character, setting,* and
plot.

A number of prosodic conventions can be discerned in
toasts. Most of them are in couplets, composed of four-stressed
lines with a varying number of unstressed syllables and fre-
quent caesuras at mid-line, establishing, as Abraham notes
(1970:99), balanced yet flexible isochronic patterns. Typical of
these characteristics is the second couplet from "Sugar Hill":

> I thought I'd like to travel, to get a taste of life,
> So I stole a car in Harlem and split New York that night.

(ll. 3–4)

Sometimes the rhyme is double, as in one couplet from "Pimping Sam":

> I could take you to my pad and give you the pipe of Gable.
> You blink your eyes and I'll have your tongue on my navel.

> (11. 37–33)

The off rhyme in these couplets is common in toasts, as it is in more traditional ballads, and indeed in many pop songs, black and white, today. *Eat:weak* forms a couplet in "Mexicana Rose," as *stick:spit* does in "The Junkie." But frequently what is off rhyme to the eye is exact rhyme to the ear when the toast is recited in black English. *Horse:boss* rhymes perfectly in "Broadway Sam," as does *order:water* in "Death Row" and *cause:drawers* in "The Ball of the Freaks."

A distinctive prosodic feature of many toasts is irregularity of rhythm. A scansion of this couplet from "Do Your Crying for the Living" would be difficult:

> On the table's your bankroll—just two dimes and a penny.
> Father Divine may not be God, but his cheap meals sure saved a many.

> (11. 11–12)

But what is irregular in print is often regular in performance: the synaloepha and other kinds of elision characteristic of black English may make the scansion of such lines perfectly possible.

Occasionally the couplet pattern is broken by the addition of another line, presumably from the sheer exuberance of the reciter. "Master of the Long-Shoe Game" has one triplet:

> My proclamation is to whores, dope fiends,
> Two-bit chislers, and mackmen supreme,
> To rich tricks who pay whores to fulfill their dreams.

> (11. 17–19)

The same rhyme forms a triplet, with internal rhyme as well, in "Pimping Sam":

> That's me, mackman supreme.
> Rich whores cream, poor whores dream.
> Some say I'm the best pimp they ever seen.

> (11. 69–71)

But not all toasts are structured in couplets. About half the lines in our collection are fitted to the classic ballad stanza— the *abcb* quatrain in alternating four- and three-stress lines— with the addition of internal rhyme in the first and third lines. This stanza from "Sporting Life" is typical:

> You forget the quote that the Christians wrote
> About honesty and fair play,
> For you can't live sweet not knowing how to cheat—
> The Game don't play that way.
>
> (11. 29–32)

"The Junkie," at 36 lines, is the shortest toast in quatrains; "The Return of Honky-Tonk Bud" the longest at 324. Toasts in couplets are generally shorter and less complex, ranging from 14 lines in "The Hustler" to 190 in "Mexicana Rose."

Perhaps the most distinctive feature that characterizes the genre is its diction. Toasts are a truly vernacular poetry. The slang, both black and white, ranges from scatology to specialized underworld argot.

One of the most obvious subjects of toast slang is personal property and its acquisition. The heroes and heroines of toasts are invariably motivated by *vines* (clothes), *shorts* (cars), and *bread* (money). Vines, shorts, and bread are the goals of the Game, and as in all games, one can *cop* (gain) or *blow* (lose).

The slang is generated particularly by the games of prostitution and drugs, both of which have highly elaborated argot. Long-Shoe Sam, the hero of "Mexicana Rose," explains that his objective in traveling to Mexico is to *pull* (recruit) some whores, which is both a personal challenge and a business venture. A woman worth such exertion must be a *stomp-down mud-kicker* (a hard-working streetwalker). The sexual slang of prostitution is profuse and vivid. The hero of "The Answer to 'The Letter' " writes of his former whore's *pot*, and the narrator of "The Fall" refers to a customer's *rod*. A whore must be capable of *turning tricks* (serving customers) in varied ways. *Giving head* (oral sex) is one—"All the long bread was made with her head" ("The Fall," 1. 117). Supplying *round-eye* (anal sex) is another—"She had good round-eye, and that's no lie" ("The Fall," 1. 121).

Toasts also contain a great deal of slang from the narcotics game. Dumbo the Junkie is so despondent when his whore runs off that he tries to commit suicide by *shooting* an *eighth* of *shit* (injecting an eighth of an ounce of heroin). Mexicana Rose promises to get *stuff* (narcotics) for Long-Shoe Sam, and he is sure that she'll keep him in kilos of *C* (cocaine). Before Andy meets Duriella du Fontaine for a date, he makes a purchase from the dealer in *snow* (cocaine).

Andy tells his own story, and that first-person dramatic perspective is typical of the genre. In some toasts, the narrators even call attention to their narrative role. "Kitty Barrett" begins with the promise, "I'll give you the wire of how I got here" (1. 2), and the narrator in "The Fall" says:

> Well, I'd like to tell of how I fell,
> And the trick fate played on me;
> So gather around, and I'll run it down
> And unravel my pedigree.
>
> (11. 5–8)

The story of "Dumbo the Junkie" is narrated in first-person participant, but it is framed by eight lines at the beginning and two at the end in first-person observer. The narrator in "Badman Dan and Two-Gun Green" introduces himself,

> I was tending bar, I'll never forget—
> It was the Bucket of Blood where the two first met.
>
> (11. 3-4)

In fact, he reports that Bad Dan "vaulted the bar and kicked *me*, the barkeep, in the ass" (1. 50).

As numerous and obtrusive as these first-person narrators are, however, nearly half of our collection, by line count, is narrated from the third-person point of view. This segment contains longer and more complicated toasts. The narrator in "Honky-Tonk Bud" is strictly impersonal, and though the narrator in its sequel, "The Return of Honky-Tonk Bud," intrudes personally in the last line, he is totally absent from the story.

Whether the narration in a toast is first person or third person, the verse always carries a distinct tone. Some narrators are so impressed by their heroes that a tone of awe is evident. This is especially true of badman toasts. But pieces like "The

Hustler," "Pimping Sam," and "Death Row" are flippant, sarcastic, or even contemptuous. In fact, the effect of some toasts depends entirely on contempt:

> Do you know what it means to wear $200 suits and $40 hats?
> ....
> No, you could never know what it means, and you never will,
> 'Cause you're one of the chumps who pay my bill.
>
> ("Do You Know What It Means?" ll. 1, 13–14)

Equally arrogant but not derisive are the narrators in "Mexicana Rose" and "Duriella du Fontaine."

Many narrators are sufficiently sophisticated to generate the appropriate tone for preceptive toasts. A sagacious note is struck by the narrator in "Sporting Life," who concludes the toast with that fatalistic resignation so pervasive in the Life:

> Just bear in mind that you must do time
>   Whenever you pull a bone:
> So don't cry in terror when you make an error—
>   Just do your bit and go home.
>
> [ll. 78–81]

The experienced pimp in "Do Your Crying for the Living" observes philosophically,

> From the crack of dawn till the setting sun,
> If you're a hustler, my man, your work's just begun.
>
> (ll. 5–6)

Two varieties of hustlers appear in toasts—the trickster, who manipulates, and the badman, who coerces. The ideal participant in the Life is neither the weak trickster—Brer Rabbit—nor the stupid badman—Brer Bear. In fact, both characters are objects of some derision in toasts as well as in folktales. In all versions of "The Signifying Monkey," for example, the titular hero is humiliated, and in some he is killed. His adversary, the lion, is in some measure a victim too, even in those versions where he kills the monkey. The ideal role is actually a synthesis of the two, but favoring cleverness—a sort of tough trickster rather than a smart badman. If there is an ideal hero in the toasts, he is the narrator of "Mexicana Rose," Long-Shoe Sam, who, when he must, knows how to handle a .44, but whose primary skill is recruiting and keeping whores. He demonstrates his prowess as a survivor. He is unflappable: his strength lies in controlling his emotions, if not his circumstances.

The simplest trickster toasts are non-narrative, like "Master of the Long-Shoe Game," where a pimp merely boasts about his achievements. "Pimping Sam," an embryonic narrative, is slightly more complicated, involving an insult-exchange. When Sweet-Loving Nell meets Sam's overtures with a threat and a catalog of her talents, he parries with "Hold on, sweetheart, with that jive-ass shit" (1. 41) and thrusts with his own list: "Sheet-shaker, cherry-breaker, baby-maker" etc. (1. 51).

Badman toasts are less typical of the Life, and in fact most of them derive from the old West narrative tradition. Yet "Bad Dan" and "Badman Dan and Two-Gun Green," though they report barroom brawls that might have come from a Western movie, do so in the language, tone, and spirit of the Life, and seem to be blends of two native folk traditions. This process of transference from one folk culture to another can be seen in many versions of the most familiar badman toast, "Stagger Lee," which derives from an old Southern ballad.

Over three-quarters of our collection have a common setting: the urban arena (the scene of the Life). Exact locations are not always identified, but in twenty-seven of our thirty-four toasts the city is unmistakably suggested by countless clues. Even the special group set in the jungle, "The Signifying Monkey" with its various elaborations and imitations, is clearly a symbolic reworking of city culture. Among toasts set in the Life, several proceed from a prison locale but only to flash back to the urban scene. "The Fall," "Kitty Barrett," and "Sugar Hill" all begin with a conventional promise to explain the narrator's presence in prison. Very few are set entirely in prison.

Yet the fact that so many heroes speak from prison or refer to it points up a significant pattern in toasts: the hero usually loses. The plots of few toasts climax in success, and even in those the gains are often trivial. To be sure, Bad Dan wins a gunfight, and Honky-Tonk Bud gets his narcotics conviction reversed, but the hero of "The Junkie" merely runs off with ten dollars, and the Pool-Shooting Monkey wins a pool game. Heroes lose their money, their whores, their freedom, even their lives. Long-Shoe Sam and the protagonist of "Duriella du Fontaine" lose women who would have made them fortunes. Honky-Tonk Bud and the narrator of "Kitty Barrett" lose their freedom, both trapped by narcotics agents posing as buyers. The protagonist of "The Fall" is denounced by his whore and jailed for pimping. The hero of "Good-Doing Wheeler" is undone by a five-to-ten year prison sentence for selling narcotics. Broadway Sam is reduced from "the big mackman" to "Sam the fag," thus losing not only his professional status and his woman but even his manhood, when his whore leads him into drug addiction and can no longer support him. Bill Skinner meets a more dramatic death, shot in the face over a game of cooncan.

Whatever the nature or degree of loss in these plots, most of them pivot on the roles of women. Some of these women are themselves valuable properties which the heroes lose; others cause losses deliberately by desertion, denunciation, or trickery. All are seen in the uniquely male perspective that informs the Life.

The Life provides a highly visible reference group, successful role models whose dash has irresistible appeal for many disaffected black youths. Whether with naturalism or caricature, toasts depict this swagger and dash without apology or defensiveness. Toasts, then, like all folk poetry, are instructive as well as entertaining. They capture the spirit of a black subculture—the Life—in our cities.

A Note on the Text

The toasts in this collection are divided broadly into narrative and non-narrative, the latter class further divided into boast and precept, as the table of contents shows. Within these classifications the material is grouped by topic wherever possible. Each toast is preceded by a headnote which describes it and relates it to others in the collection; at the end of each headnote there is information on the sources, giving the place, time, and informant. The first appearance of a performer—all of whom are listed on page 9—contains information on his age and background. An index of titles and first lines has also been provided, on page 203.

The glossary on pages 175–192 should clarify any word or phrase that is unfamiliar, and each entry is followed by references back to all the appearances of that word or phrase in the texts, listed alphabetically by title. Thus this section may serve as both a glossary and a concordance to the toasts in this volume, providing the folklorist with explanations of the language and the dialectologist with examples of usage.

No attempt has been made to present these toasts "in dialect." It would obviously have been impracticable to employ a narrow phonetic transcription, and anything less would have been both unscientific and patronizing. Practice varies in this matter, but most collectors, like Abrahams,

Labov, and Jackson, have used some sort of modified phonetic spellings in presenting toasts, and the results add neither to readability nor to precision. To use an apostrophe to indicate the substitution of the *n*-sound for the *ng*-sound in words ending in *ing* merely underlines the obvious; both the rhyme and common knowledge tell the reader that black English "drops the g" in these words. Nothing useful is added by spelling "signifying" with -*in'* when it rhymes with "lion."

The same applies to the suppression of the *r*-sound after vowels; writing "ho" for "whore" in an otherwise conventional orthography, as the Milners (1972) have done, is distracting, and to carry such a practice out one would have to write "do" for "door," "ah" for "are," and so forth.

And even if some sort of patronizing Uncle Remus style had been attempted in collecting the material presented here, there was too much diversity of pronunciation in the original performances for a clear transcription. Black English is, after all, not a uniform dialect; these verses were recited by people from widely scattered places, speaking differently enough to have necessitated quite different systems of transcriptions to render their pronunciations accurately. Since such renderings could not be done consistently without loss of clarity, it seemed best to employ conventional spelling throughout.

These texts, then, are all "original language versions" merely spelled conventionally. No word has been suppressed, supplied, or altered.

The Toasts

NARRATIVES
BOASTS and PRECEPTS

Narratives

Just as most folklorists have sweepingly identified toasts as "narratives," most reciters tend to think of the story-toast as typical. Surely it is the best and most elaborated form.

The stories to be found in toasts range widely, but all can be seen to come, directly or indirectly, from the experience of the Life. Even when they are fantasies or adaptations of material from outside sources, something of the black urban experience underlies the thinking and language which inform them and identifies them clearly as products of their unique milieu.

THE SIGNIFYING MONKEY

Perhaps the best known of all toasts, "The Signifying Monkey" is the prototype of an interrelated series of jungle poems. Though these pieces may seem to be mere animal stories, they are, in fact, elaborate metaphors for the urban jungle. Roger D. Abrahams, whose book *Deep Down in the Jungle* takes its name from the first line of "The Signifying Monkey," has dealt with these poems at length (Abrahams, 1970C:142–57), and Bruce Jackson has devoted an entire section of his *Get Your Ass in the Water and Swim Like Me* (Jackson, 1974:161–79) to them. Both provide excellent summaries of the literature on the subject.

These animal tales are unique among toasts in setting and characters, but the first of them has a special quality which sets it apart from the other two: alone among the protagonists of toasts, the Signifying Monkey is motivated by sheer mischief. It is not, however, a playful spirit which motivates him to trick the lion; the depth of his hostility is evident from the gloating spirit in which he reviews his victim's defeat (11. 51–64). He may be compared with the European Reynard or Uncle Remus' Brer Rabbit; his humor thinly veils the hatred he feels. It is the classic hatred of the weak for the strong. The lion's title, King of the Jungle, and his "rah rah shit" drive the monkey to his actions.

In this personal malice the monkey differs from other trickster heroes in the toasts and thus may provide a link with the African origins of the series. The clever pimp who represents the typical descendant of the Signifying Monkey is much too pragmatic, much too concerned with either survival or acquisition, to indulge himself in the luxury of cruelty for its own sake. But the great popularity of the toast reveals the affinity

21

that people in the Life feel for its curiously unattractive hero. In some versions the monkey slips again and the lion kills him; but in most, as here, he triumphs and lives to signify another day.

"The Signifying Monkey" is so well known that a public recitation of it takes on something of the character of a sing-along, the audience following the familiar narrative with their lips. The version given here was delivered from a cell in Attica Prison in 1962, other inmates on the gallery prompting the speaker as he faltered or joining him in delivering the most popular lines. It was recited by Lou, a black petty thief from New York, who reported that he first heard it as a child in the early 1950's. Lou considered toasts to be exclusively a young man's entertainment, claiming never to have heard one recited "outside" by anyone over thirty; but then, it is unlikely that Lou had ever socialized with anyone over thirty outside. He reports that he got it from "the kids in the neighborhood" on the upper east side of Manhattan.

The Signifying Monkey

Deep down in the jungle where the tall grass grows
Lived the signifyingest monkey that the world knows.

He was up in a tree, just snoring a bit,
When he thought he'd come up with some of his shit.

Now down on the ground in a great big ring
Lived a bad-ass lion who knew he was king.

The signifying monkey spied the lion one day
And said, "I heard something 'bout you down the way.

"There's a big motherfucker lives over there,
And the way he talks would curl your hair.   10

"From what he said he can't be your friend,
'Cause he said if your two asses meet, yours is sure
                          to bend.
"This burly motherfucker says your mammy's a whore
And your sister turns tricks on the cabin floor.

"And he talked 'bout your wife in a hell of a way,
Said the whole jungle fucked her just the other day.

"If he said that 'bout my bitch, he'd have to pay.
I'd whip his ass all motherfucking day."

Now the lion jumped up full of rage
Like a ditty bopper ready to rampage.   20

He ran through the jungle like death on a breeze,
Knocking all the coconuts off the trees.

He came on a hippo, bathing in a pond
And said, "Come out, motherfucker, the show is on."

Hippo said, "Get your wires straight 'fore you get me.
The one you want is behind that tree."

He dug the elephant behind a pine
And said, "Come on, motherfucker, your ass is mine."

The elephant looked out from the corner of his eyes
And said, "Ain't you better pick on someone your size?"   30

Old lion jumped up with a mighty pass,
But elephant knocked him dead on his ass.

He romped and stomped, and he fucked up his face,
Kicked him so hard he knocked his asshole out of place.

They fought all night and half the next day,
And I still don't know how the lion drug his ass away.

But back he came, more dead than alive,
And the monkey came up with more of his jive.

The monkey had been watching from his tree all the while
And started signifying in true monkey style.   40

He said, "Hey, Mr. Lion, you sure look sad.
That cocksucker must've really been bad.

"When you left here you were yelling like a pup.
Now look at you—you're all fucked up.

"Ha, ha! That old elephant sure gave you hell.
Why, he whipped your poor ass to a very well.

"You look like a whore with the seven-year itch.
'King of the Jungle!' Ain't you a bitch!

"And don't tell me you didn't get beat,
'Cause my bitch and I had a ringside seat.   50

"Every time I'm up here copping a bit,
Here you come with that rah rah shit.

"Now go on, get your ass out from under my tree
Before I swing on over your head and pee."

The monkey jumped up, down and around,
Till his foot missed a limb and his ass hit the ground.

Lion took off with a hell of a roar,
His tail popping like a Colt .44.

Like a bolt of lightning and a streak of heat
The lion was on his ass with all four feet.   60

The monkey looked up with tears in his eyes
And said, "God *damn*, Mr. Lion, I apologize!"

Lion said, "No use your pleading and crying,
'Cause I'm going to put an end to your signifying.

"This signifying's got to stop,
And I'm tearing you up from asshole to top."

Monkey saw that he couldn't get away,
So he had to think of something to say.

Lion said, "Mr. Monkey, make your last request."
Monkey said, "Get your feet off my motherfucking chest.   70

"I know you think you're raising hell
Just because you caught me when I slipped and fell,

"But just let me get my ass off the ground and my balls
                    out the sand,
And I'll whip your ass like a natural man.

"If you let me up like a fighting man should,
I'll romp your old ass all over these woods."

Now such a bold challenge the lion'd never had,
And it made the old lion fighting mad.

So he backed off ready for a fight,
And the signifying monkey jumped clear out of sight.   80

As far as the average eye could see,
The signifying monkey landed in the highest tree.

Saying, "Mr. Lion, Mr. Lion, don't you know,
That's the bullshit that made the green grass grow.

"Mr. Lion, Mr. Lion, you thought you were king,
But I found out you weren't a *God* damned thing.

"Down on the ground I'll treat you like a brother,
But up in this tree you're a no-good motherfucker.

"And I swear if you ever fuck with me again,
I'll go deep in the jungle and get my elephant friend."   90

Then he laughed and called as he swung away,
"I'll live to signify another day!"

The Signifying Monkey II

Untitled except as the second "Signifying Monkey," this little sequel identifies the setting more clearly as the city: the simian hero hears the events of the preceding toast in a bar, the jungle creatures bet on the fight, and the bear's costume (11. 23–24) is clearly inappropriate to the African jungle.

The story is in a sense a counterweight to that of its predecessor and accordingly reflects more directly the practical wisdom of life in the city: "The Signifying Monkey" is a tale of successful mischief, clearly in the tradition of the picaresque, but its sequel is essentially an exemplum. The monitory note sounded in the last line is a version of the Life axiom "Don't let your mouth overload your ass"—don't start anything you're not man enough to finish.

Doe Eye, the young burglar mentioned in the Introduction, followed Lou's recitation in Attica with this version of "the other 'Signifying Monkey' " during the same 1962 session. A black about twenty, Doe Eye claimed to have been in the Life on a small scale, with an occasional dope deal and a girlfriend bringing him in a little money, but his conviction was for burglary. He himself never touched narcotics, fearing its effects, but he used to sit in on sessions where it was taken, and reported that he had heard this toast at one of them in Harlem.

The Signifying Monkey II

Now old monkey's cousin, Chicken Shit Baboon,
Was standing at a bar, humming a tune,

Sipping his beer and having a ball,
When he heard the news of his cousin's downfall.

He looked in the mirror with fire in his eyes
And said, "That old yellow-ass lion is about my size.

"Give me a shot of whiskey and a tall glass of gin
'Cause I got a long way to go and a short time to make
it in."

He bid all his friends goodbye and said, "It's
time to go,
'Cause I'm going to whip that lion's ass just
a little more."   10

When he reached the jungle, it was just about night,
And his friends had gathered to see the fight.

They were all betting the lion couldn't win,
Seeing the condition the poor bastard was in.

The little old rabbit who watched the fight from
the grass
Saw the elephant when he stomped the lion's ass.

He jumped up from the grass with his gold in his hand
And said, "Show me a sucker and I'll bet him a grand."

The old monkey, who was wise now, you see,
Said, "I'll bet that grand, and I'll raise you three."   20

Old bear was a man of justice and right,
So it fell to him to announce the fight.

He was hard as lard and stashed 'way back,
Wore a diamond on each toe and a three-button sack.

He said, "Over in this corner we have you-know-who,
And over here's Chicken Shit—he's a bad man too."

To everyone it was plain to see
That Tarzan would act as referee.

Now old bear stepped out, and baboon stepped in,
And that's when the odds jumped from four to ten.   30

Baboon turned his head to take a spit,
And lion was on him like stink on a shit.

He knocked out all his teeth and stomped on his face,
Broke both his jaws and pulled his balls out of place.

All the audience turned their head,
'Cause they knew old Chicken Shit would soon be dead.

Then the lion called out from the middle of the ring,
"Anyone else think he's the motherfucking king?"

Old monkey saw his cousin laying on the grass
And said, "You were a good kid, but you overloaded   40
                    your ass."

So if any of you boys get big, bad, and bold,
Never jump on more than your ass can hold.

THE POOL-SHOOTING MONKEY

A kind of imitation, if not actually a parody, of the prototype of the jungle pieces, "The Pool-Shooting Monkey" brings the urban setting into still sharper focus and demonstrates the essential compatibility of the series with the urban poems. The baboon and the monkey have here lost all traces of the jungle and acquired every element of the Life: the flashy clothes and jewelry, the marijuana, the inevitable Cadillac, and even a car full of prostitutes. The transition from Africa to Harlem is complete.

"The Pool-Shooting Monkey" was taken down at the same recitation session as the two preceding it here. It was recited twice, once in so broken a version that others on the gallery complained and it was cut off midway, the reciter hooted into silence. At last, after some noisy argument, an approved version was delivered by Washington, as presented here. Washington at thirty had spent almost all of his life in prison. He was serving time for manslaughter and had been in Attica for six or seven years already. He reported later that he had first learned "The Pool-Shooting Monkey," along with most of the toasts he knew, in "the kid joints," the various New York State correctional institutions for juvenile offenders, in which he had spent his youth.

The Pool-Shooting Monkey

Deep down in the jungle where it's always dark,
The animals had a poolroom where the baboon was
                    the shark.

With his long pointy shoes and his hat pulled close
                    on his head,
Everyone called him the Razor's Edge.

MEXICANA ROSE

Though set in a Mexican border town, this poem deals with
New York pimps solidly placed in the Life; indeed, even the
Mexican titular heroine speaks its language after her opening
line. The story exemplifies one of the recurring toast plots: the
loss of a profitable, or potentially profitable, whore.

Señorita Bonita, or Rosita Espinosa as she is known in some
versions, is a classic figure; she typifies the ideal whore whose
death or defection brings the narrator-hero down for a while.
The tragedy here is clearly not hers; it is Sam's.

The popularity of this toast is attested by the frequency with
which its characters appear or are referred to in others. Rose is
mentioned in "The Return of Honky-Tonk Bud" (1. 90), and
her cousin shows up in "Duriella du Fontaine" (1. 156). Both
the narrator and his sidekick attend the ball of the freaks ("Ball
of the Freaks," 1. 27) and are claimed as students by a boasting
hustler ("Master of the Long-Shoe Game," 1. 13). Smitty at-
tends Honky-Tonk Bud's trial ("Honky-Tonk Bud," 1. 100).

The variant title "Mexicali Rose," by which the poem is
probably best known, presumably comes from the popular
song of that name. It does not appear logical, for in virtually all
versions the story is set "down in old Sonora."

The version of "Mexicana Rose" that follows comes from
Sing Sing Prison, where toasts were often recited in the recreation yard. It was taken down in 1954 from a performance by
Eddie, a black in his middle forties who boasted of having
been in every prison in New York State and at least one county
jail in each of thirty other states as well. A burglar by preference, Eddie had done time for a wide variety of small-scale
crimes and was in Sing Sing for aggravated assault. Wise to
the ways of prison, he was always able to get good jobs and
was working at this time in the hospital. Despite a New York
City high school education, Eddie was almost completely illit-
erate, and he ascribed his excellent verbal memory to that fact;
he had to be good at remembering, he pointed out, because he
couldn't write things down. This talent had several advan-

tages for Eddie. It made him a welcome guest at social functions because of the many toasts he could keep in his head, and as a numbers runner he didn't have to carry any incriminating evidence.

Eddie said that he had heard toasts in all the many prisons where he had spent time but that "Mexicana Rose" had been in his repertoire since his early childhood in the Brownsville section of Brooklyn, where, he asserted, "Everybody knows it."

Mexicana Rose

Way down in old Sonora where the pot grows tall,
Vultures fly the skies, and the rattlesnakes crawl.

Scorpions creep over dead men's bones,
And coyotes yelp in blood-curdling tones.

It was in this hot, dry desert waste
That I first came face to face

With the queen of all the whores,
Señorita Bonita, the Mexicana Rose.

I was traveling with my partner, Cocaine Smitty,
On our way to pull some whores in Mexico City.   10

Now we were big-time pimps from the New York scene,
And believe me, Jim, we were both real clean.

I had a sharkskin vine in a powder blue,
Black wingtips from Bendette's, sparkling new,

My shirts were from Brooks'; my socks cost a pound;
I wore solid gold cufflinks—I knew I was down.

I wore a hat from Disney with a fifty-dollar tag,
And my snakeskin billfold was loaded with swag.

My man Smitty was also pressed,
And looked real tough, I must confess.   20

He had on a three-hundred-dollar vine
Straight from the Phil Kronfield line.

His shirt and tie were from Edmond Clapp,
And he sported a P. Santini cap.

Now his cufflinks looked like they cost a grand,
But I peeped the back; they said "Made in Japan."[1]

Well, pulling some whores was our pimping motto,
As we pushed toward the border in my black Eldorado.

When we reached the border, we had to give our name,
Long-Shoe Sam and Smitty Cocaine.   30

When we reached Sonora we needed some gas,
So I pulled into a station and said, "Fill 'er up fast."

Then we stepped into Pancho's for a bite to eat,
But when we dug the waitress, our knees got weak.

She was dressed like a native in sombrero and jeans
And said, "Qué pasa, señores? Tamales or beans?"

"There's just one thing I want," said Smitty, "and I'll
                    give you a clue.
It's the best dish in the house, and it seems to be you."

She had eyes like diamonds, big, black, and bold,
And her soft smooth skin was the color of gold.   40

Her lips ran like a cool mountain well
That showed all the fire and brimstone of hell.

---

[1]A recurring device in toasts. See "The Letter," 11. 47–48.

Her hair was long and shiny with a glare,
And she had a body that would make Jane Russell stop
and stare.

Her lips, hips, and kiester were so shapely and fine
Smitty went berserk and screamed, "She's *got* to be mine!"

He said, "Come here, baby, and tell me your name.
My name is Smitty, they call me Cocaine."

Then he pulled her aside and showed her his dough
And said, "I'm taking you back to be my whore."   50

For a minute I thought the bitch was going for his spiel,
Till she shot back, "Creep, are you for real?

"Cocaine Smitty from New York City,
For a half-ass pimp you sure talk shitty.

"What makes you think I want to be your whore?
You'd take me to New York, and then where would I go?

"All you pimps come down here talking that shit;
Last time it was a horn-blowing chump named Stitt.[2]

"He was a drug-using cat who didn't have a dime,
But I'd go back with him before I'd fall for your line.   60

"Sure you'll take me to New York, buy me rings and
fancy clothes;
But I don't need your shit, lame, I'm the Mexicana Rose!

"I want to *own* New York, and you're not that slick."
"Here, take my money," cried Smitty, "and let me be
your trick."

"Be my trick? Why you insult my pride.
Go hit on one of them Indian bitches selling blankets outside."

[2]Sonny Stitt, alto and tenor saxophonist, born 1925.

By this time I'd moved in to give this bitch a closer
                    observation,
So I told Smitty, "Beat it, you must be beat for
                    conversation.

"I thought you were a thoroughbred, my ace man,
But I find you're a comical stud, funnier than
                    Charlie Chan.   70

"I thought you were a mackman, a master at the Game;
But I peeped your hole card, you're a funny-time lame.

"You wait till I get back to the Big Apple and tell all
                    the crowd
How you come down to Mexico sounding all loud,

"Hit on a bitch to be your whore,
And turned stone-cold trick when she said no!"

"Ha!" said Smitty, coming up from behind.
"Do you think your game is stronger than mine?"

"Not only do I think it's stronger," I said with a jerk,
"But step aside, creep, and watch a master at work."   80

I sat at the table, crossed my knees,
And said, "Waitress, two tequilas, please."

When I pulled out some pot and Rose said,. "Yeah!"
I dug right away that she was no square.

As we sat there gaily blowing on our hemp,
I whispered, "Rose, darling, let me be your pimp.

"I've had queens, stallions, all kinds of a whore,
But I've never had a whore like you before.

"I won't treat you like no lady, or any fancy queen;
I'll take all your money and treat you real mean.   90

"There's not going to be a whole lot of rings and
fancy clothes,
But you better make me more money than all them
other whores.

" 'Cause if you come up weak, I'm going for your knot and gut
And throw you in the gutter like an ordinary slut.

"But if you follow the rules according to the Game,
We'll soon be on Easy Street with much money
and cocaine."

"Damn," said Rose, "I thought I was a way-out bitch.
And here you shoot me a prop like I was a witch!

"I go for you, Sam, I think you're boss,
But don't think you can ever put me in a cross.   100

"Before I say yes or before I say no,
Let's go in the game room and see what you know."

First she engaged me in a nine-ball game,
But that sharp-shooting bitch won every frame.

Next cards, which wasn't my stick;
Not that my game was weak, but hers was so goddam slick.

But when we came to craps, that was a different story;
That's when I came out of my slump and went into
my glory.

I shot five-two for seven and five-six for eleven,
And from there on in I was really in heaven.   110

Now I shook the dice and threw them on the floor.
They turned up ten—a six and a four.

Rose said, "Let's play for higher stakes—my body
                    and soul
Against your black Eldorado trimmed in pure gold."

Rose picked up the dice and shot them one-two;
She shrugged and sat, 'cause she knew she had blew.

Now I shivered and trembled, more dead than alive,
Till I made my point the hard way, five and five.

"I have lost," said Rose, "and now I'm yours,
But I'm not going to be like the rest of your whores.   120

"I'll make a whole lot of money for you, 'cause hustling's
                    in my blood,
And because I go for you and think you're a way-out stud.

"I'll take numbers, cop stuff, steal booze or anything
            of value from three-cent stamps to rockets,
I'll play the Murphy to the point of death, and I'll
                    even pick pockets.

"I'll rob trains and banks and lots of other things,
And take the weight for narcotics rings."

"Damn!" I said. "Now this is *it*.
This broad is mine, and she talks a whole lot of shit.

"She'll keep me in kilos of C and in the champagne
By turning tricks and beating lames.   130

"Never again will I have to pawn my clothes
As long as I have a bitch like the Mexicana Rose.

"She'll be the best of the hustlers, the queen of
                    the whores,
The pride of New York, the Mexicana Rose."

Now we'd forgotten Smitty, who was digging all the while,
Or else we'd have dug his madman smile.

Cocaine's mind had snapped with hate,
And he reached in his pocket for his .38.

He said, "If I can't have this bitch for my very own,
I'll kill both you chumps and head back home.   140

"Say your prayers, Long-Shoe. You're the first to go."
But Rose jumped in and said, "Hell, no!

"Kill me, creep, but not Long-Shoe Sam,
For I love him madly, he's my motherfucking man.

"He's a thoroughbred, my kind of guy,
And just to prove it, I'm ready to die."

"Quiet," said Smitty, "or I'll draw you on a bead."
"Faggot," said Rose, "your heart's a mustard seed."

Now what Rose said was true, Smitty didn't want
                              to fight,
But his finger pulled the trigger just out of
                              pure fright.   150

The bullet struck Rose high on her head,
And she toppled over backwards, damn near dead.

Cocaine Smitty stood there stunned,
Then he dropped his pistol and started to run.

But before he got within ten feet of the door
I dropped him with a cap from my Colt .44.

I shot him in the ass, and I shot him in the teeth,
And I said, "Now, creep, you ain't got no beef."

Now Rose was in her death throb and started to twitch.
She said, "I'm sorry, pretty papa, I could have made
                                   you rich."   160

She choked a minute and said, "So long."
Her eyelids fluttered, and she was gone.

Well, I took her body back to New York City
With the cigar-box remains of Cocaine Smitty.

I gave her a way-out funeral and didn't spare no cash.
I buried her in satin lace and an ermine sable sash.

I gave her the Queen Victoria crown and the
                              Cinderella shoes
And hired Count Basie to play the "St. Louis Blues."

That's the end of my toast, there's no more to be said
Except that on her tombstone it simply read: 170

"Here lies the body of Mexicana Rose,
Destined to be the queen of the whores.

"She died young, much before her time,
Before she had a chance to make her man a dime.

"She was shot in the head by Smitty Cocaine,
A notorious shortstop and a practical lame.

"But she died brave, protecting her man,
Dean of all mackmen, Long-Shoe Sam."

DURIELLA DU FONTAINE

Like her sister south of the border, Duriella is a dream whore who would have brought her man a fortune if fate had not intervened. Duriella's "copper" skin, blue eyes, and blonde hair (11. 32–33) show the high value placed on white standards of beauty in women at the time of this version, which seems, from its references to Cuban cigars and jet planes, to have originated in the middle 50's.

Two distinctive features characterize the heroine of this toast: more than a mere sex machine, she is herself a "cold-blooded mack" who reverses the usual rôles by schooling her pimp (1. 97); and although she accepts the position of his "own true bitch" (1. 90), she earns that rarest of Life commodities, a pimp's love (1. 131). The elegiac note on which the poem ends suggests a romantic spirit seldom encountered in toasts.

Doe Eye performed this version of "Duriella" in Attica in 1962 for an audience most of whose members already knew it. It was very popular, he said, in Harlem, where he had heard it often.

Duriella du Fontaine

I was standing around in the heart of town
    In the middle of the square,
Waiting for my man, 'cause I'd made a plan
    To cop some reefer there.

Now I was fly and fairly high,
    Just standing there digging the whores,
When up drove my man, Good-Doing Van,
    In his brand new Ninety-Eight Olds.

Van had a straw, a Corona Corona in his jaw,
    A beige suit looking real quilty,   10
Shoes made of one piece that came from Greece—
    He was dressed to make Latins feel guilty.

I was also pressed in some of the best,
    But I couldn't compare with Van.
My taste was as good as his, but the reason is
    Van was a big money man.

He got out, looked all about,
    And started in to speak,
When from the side, with a sexy stride,
    Came a broad that looked some boss freak.   20

She wore a white chemise dress, one of the best,
    And her hair was a glossy blonde;
Her skin copper hue and her eyes a sky blue,
    I could see she was real down.

She had ruby lips and big swinging hips
    And a kiester that was real fine.
She didn't need to hunt for someone to suck her cunt,
    'Cause I'd do it any old time.

I spoke to Van and shook her hand
    And asked if this was his honey.   30
With a bit of a sigh he gave this reply:
    "She's anyone's who has some money.

"She's real down, known all around;
    Playing is her stick.
Duriella du Fontaine is this chick's name,
    But be careful, for this bitch is slick.

"I've seen this broad work, she's really no jerk;
    She's cool and uses her head.
She's a cold-blooded mack from a long way back
    And can definitely get to the bread."   40

"Look, fellows," said D., "I'm starved as can be."
    So we agreed on a boss feed that night.
We went to a joint down the street which was real elite,
    And this was my first real flight.

We were players, it's true, with ribbons of blue,
    But clean as the board of health.
No cop could tip, 'cause we were too hip:
    We painted a picture of wealth.

A captain named Abel showed us to our table
    And brought us back some wine,   50
Refreshing as cocaine from the castles of Spain,
    Vintage 1879.

We ate hummingbirds' hearts and other rare parts,
    Topped off with a seven-inch steak;
Grand à la king with butterfly wings
    And a salad that took three chefs to make.

We had bumblebee legs and peacock eggs
    Steamed over leaves from Peru.
An hour was spent over creme de menthe,
    As we sat admiring the view.   60

Now the time we were dining, Van was unwinding
    All of my pedigree.
As we smoked a cigarette and Van paid the debt,
    I knew she was pinning me.

"Look here, fella," said Duriella,
    "I'd like to see you again.
Why not come around to my part of town,
    Say, Saturday night about ten."

Saturday night I got fly and went on by
    To see Miss du Fontaine.   70
I stopped off at Joe, the dealer in snow,
    And copped a bag of cocaine.

I got to her pad, which was some kind of bad,
    Filled with a real nice scent,
With a three-inch carpet that came from the market
    Somewhere in the Orient.

The hi-fi was wailing, but I was failing;
    I just couldn't take to this queen.
She dug my feet was cold, so she took hold
    And gave me some pot, light green.   80

She put C on her thumb, painted my gum
    And gave me some wine to sip.
You should have heard her purr as I looked at her
    And painted her gums and lips.

She looked me dead in the eye, and without no lie,
    Here's just what that fine chick said:
"I dig you, Andy; as a pair we'd be dandy.
    Like cocaine, you go to my head.

"If you'll be my man, I'll comb the land
    And be your own true bitch.   90
But there are times you must lend me to other men,
    And with their money I'll make you rich."

Now, you know where I'm at; I really bought that
    And led her on off to bed.
Me and this queen made love supreme,
    And I flipped when she gave me some head.

For a month or more I was schooled by this whore.
    It was like a wonder dream.
I really learned well, 'cause I can't begin to tell
    Of how this bitch could scheme.   100

Then one day in bed, "Andy, honey," she said,
    Today's to be our first big day."
We got our heads bad and left the pad,
    And I went to the street to play.

It was in the Celebrity Club I made my first big rub
    With a game called the Japanese fan.
I caught me a fool and took him real cool
    For a short and eight solid grand.

He was a fag, and so I had to shag,
    And D. didn't dig the show.   110
But she soon came at ease when I showed the eight G's
And poured it out on the floor.

"Andy, honey," said she, "I'm glad you're with me.
    Van said you were a thoroughbred."
But the truth of the thing, this was my only big sting,
    Though now and then I scored some light bread.

But my slick chick knew every trick,
    And with her the cash rolled in.
We lived real hearty, life was a party,
    With money, narcotics, and gin.   120

Our pad was the best, and we both stayed real pressed;
    The tricks would come and go.
We stayed real high and kept ourselves fly,
    For in hustling D. could always make dough.

One night in bed, "Andy, honey," she said,
    "Money I've got plenty of.
So you needn't give me rings, mink coats, and such things.
    Just give me the strength of your love."

Now this really wigged me, 'cause I couldn't quite see
    This fast whore being romantically up tight.   130
But I was in love, too, so what could we do
    But treat each other right?

Then one night about one we were out having fun
    In a club called the Isle of Joy,
When we met Dixie Fair, multi-millionaire
    And international playboy.

"Look, fellow," said Fair, "who's that fine babe there,
    Wearing that engine-red dress?
I'll pay you a fee if you'll introduce her to me."
    I did, and Duriella did the rest.   140

That night in bed, "Andy, honey," she said,
    "I know I can take Dixie's dough.
But you'll have to lay for me real patiently
    Down in sunny old Mexico.

"I don't want you 'round when I take off this clown
    And snare him into my den.
Then I'll come back to you and always be true,
    And we'll never have to hustle again."

I took my clothes off the hook, took out my bank book,
    And made love for the rest of the day.   150
At nine that night I took off on my flight
    In a furious TWA.

My stay wasn't bad; I had a boss pad,
    And there was plenty of fabulous whores.
I pulled Carmen Trista, who was big in the kiester
    And a cousin of Mexican Rose.

Though the climate was hot, there was plenty of pot,
    And the tequila was dynamite.
I laid in the cut on Carmen's big butt
    And kept her on her knees all night.   160

And then one day the mailman came that way
    With a New York cablegram.
"Andy, papa," it stated, "I'm glad you have waited,
    For I've really hit a grand slam.

"I'm leaving today and I'm on my way,
    Arriving Jet Comet three.
Buenos Aires at four, sorry cannot say more,
    Love from your woman, D."

Carmen bathed me in milk. I put on my gray silk
    And downed me some ice-cold wine.   170
I bought a *New York News* that rocked me in my shoes
    When I dug this bold headline:

"MR. DIXIE FAIR, MULTI-MILLIONAIRE,
    COMMITTED SUICIDE AND DIED.
HE LEFT ALL HIS GAME TO A MISS DU FONTAINE,
    WHO WAS SLATED TO BE HIS BRIDE."

I fought to stay calm after this atom bomb,
    But I grinned from ear to ear.
I knew my luck had turned as soon as I learned
    All those big bucks would soon be here.   180

I lit a smoke and made a joke
    With the man who drove the cab.
I hummed a tune and watched the moon
    As I calmly paid the tab.

We got to the field, and again I reeled
    As I heard the loudspeaker roar:
"Jet Comet three went down at sea
    A hundred miles from shore.

"Reports all state that the hand of fate
    Has not left one alive.   190
The plane was loaded, and when it exploded,
    No one had a chance to survive.

"A young lady gasped as she breathed her last.
    'Tell Andy Gray,' she sighed,
'I'd have been his true bitch who'd have made him rich.'
    Then she coughed up some blood and died."

Well, I'll pull through, like all down dudes do,
    And go on playing the Game.
But I know for me there never could be
    Another bitch like Duriella du Fontaine.   200

KITTY BARRETT

Never very far from the Life is the specter of prison, which waits around the corner to claim the careless, the inept, and the unlucky. A prison sentence is a normal part of every career: "Just bear in mind that you must do time / Whenever you pull a bone," the player is reminded in "Sporting Life" (ll. 77–78). Many first-person toasts are conceived as spoken in prison and employ a beginning formula in which the narrator promises to explain how he came there: "I'd like to tell of how I fell" ("The Fall," 1. 5); "I'm now about to tell you why I really came to jail" ("Sugar Hill," 1. 2). Going to and returning from prison is an important element in the plots of many others.

Probably based on true experience, "Kitty Barrett" is the only toast in this collection whose subject is definitely identifiable. Kitty Barrett was a legendary officer in the New York Police Department's narcotics squad, and many a dealer can attest to her ingenuity. Descriptions of her vary—her blonde hair mentioned here (1. 13) was probably a disguise—but everyone agrees that she was as beautiful as she was courageous and clever, and she continued to operate as a successful narco long after she became known in the city. The poem can be dated from the late 40's to the middle 50's.

Slim, who recited this toast in Auburn in 1966, claimed to have had personal experience with its heroine. He was serving time for narcotics sale and spoke with great authority on the personnel of the New York City narco squad.

Kitty Barrett

Say, my man, lend me your ear,
And I'll put you wise on how I got here.

It was five years ago this very day
That that stuff-playing whore came my way.

Now I had a corner just like the rollers got a beat,
Right on Eighth Avenue and a Hundred and
                    Fifteenth Street.

I was standing on the corner, just as fly as I could be,
Selling boss smack to every dope fiend I could see,

When this queen rolled on the scene and began to pin.
With one look at her I could tell she was pure sin.   10

She tipped up in front of me, and then she stopped
And said, "Hey, pretty daddy, do you know where I
                    can cop?"

I said, "Hi, Miss Blonde Lady, who might you be?
Step a little closer and let me dig your pedigree."

She said, "I'm a stone dope fiend and a turned-out whore,
And I'll beat a trick's stash while he's putting the key
                    in the door."

I said, "Name some of the fellows you know who
                    are down."
She said, "Fats, Count, Lucky, and Elmira Brown."

I said, "All those people live up the way."
She said, "I know, but they moved downtown the   20
                    other day."

Now what that chick said didn't strike me as odd.
How was I to know she was on the narcotics squad?

So I reached in my slide and came out with two boss threes
And said, "Here, girl, go to the shithouse and get the
                    weakness out your knees."

The whore moved off, her ass jumping smooth as lard,
And I just laid back and let my dick get hard.

When the whore came out the shithouse, nodding and
                    staggering back,
I yelled down the bar, "Vodka and orange juice, Jack."

She said, "You know, a pretty daddy like you should be
                    pushing a Cadillac car,
Pissing imported champagne and shitting caviar.   30

"You need a good-doing bitch like me to boost
                    your stable,
'Cause a whore like me looks good in mink or sable."

I said, "Say, Mommy, where are you from?" She said,
                    "I'm from the land of play,
And if I don't make three bills, then I had a bad day."

Now by this time my dick was really hard for this
                    old queen,
And all the pimps and numbers men were digging the scene.

So I decided to show the whore how big time I was; so
                    I rushed her to my pad
And laid on the table all the stuff that I had.

Before I knew what happened, the whore took her pocketbook
                    and went to my brain
With a shot that floored me like a shot of cocaine.   40

She slapped me and kicked me and threw me upside the wall,
Pulled her pistol and said she'd waste me if I moved
                    a muscle at all.

I sat in a chair and let my head shake for a while,
And that's when the whore came out with a way-out style.

She said, "Pretty daddy, don't take it so hard.
My name is Kitty Barrett of the New York Narco Squad."

Well, baby, I got busted, just like that.
So I hope this toast helps you when they give you your hat.

HONKY-TONK BUD

A more elaborate version of the Kitty Barrett story—narcotics dealer trapped by agent posing as buyer—"Honky-Tonk Bud" shows us a good deal about the positive values of the Life. Bud is a far cry from the Signifying Monkey; although this is a story of his defeat, he emerges as a hero. Popular in his community, clever at his trade, stoical in disaster, he accepts his arrest, "so grave and unjust," with dignity and spirit. Whether or not he was really "a master of the long-shoe game," as the D.A. tries to make out, is not clear in the text; he denies it, and his initial appearance does not suggest it. But he represents all the virtues of the Life: dapper, cool, contemptuous of the society which condemns him, he goes to his fate with *élan*.

Besides the long sequel which follows this poem here, three other toasts contain references to Bud: "Konky Mohair" (11. 99–100), "Master of the Long-Shoe Game" (1. 16), and "Wise Egg" (1. 14).

Michael Agar (1971) has analyzed "Honky-Tonk Bud" at length; his version, collected in Kentucky, differs only slightly from that presented here.

"Honky-Tonk Bud" is a well-known toast and was heard from both blacks and whites. This version came from Duke, who is mentioned in the Introduction. It was recited in Auburn in 1964.

Honky-Tonk Bud

Honky-Tonk Bud, the hipcat stud,
　　Stood digging a game of pool.
His pants weren't bagging and he wasn't bragging,
　　'Cause he knew he was looking cool.

He was choked up tight in a white-on-white
　　And a cocoa front that was down.
A candy-striped tie hung down to his fly,
　　And he sported a gold-dust crown.

It was the eighteenth frame of a nine-ball game,
    And Bud stood digging the play,   10
When with an idle shrug he suddenly dug
    A strange cat coming his way.

It was a beat-up cat with a funny-time hat
    That looked to be five years old;
He had a mussed-up vine and needed a shine
    And shivered as though he was cold.

The other guys all dropped their eyes,
    'Cause he looked like an ordinary flunky.
But Bud was swift; he looked up and sniffed
    And dug the cat was a junkie.   20

The hipcat pinned as the stud moved in
    And asked for a cat named Joe.
But Joe wasn't around, 'cause his bags was down,
    And he'd gone to shop for dough.

"I'm Honky-Tonk Bud," said the hipcat stud,
    "From over on Eighth Avenue.
Say, you look sick, like you need a fix.
    Perhaps I can do some solids for you.

"So if you want to cop, then let's talk shop.
    I'm hip and can help you score.   30
I've got the best in the East and the West
    At my pad. Need I say more?"

The chump looked down with a halfway frown
    As if to make up his mind.
"I'm leery," he said, "but I've got the bread,
    And I want the best stuff I can find.

"Now I ain't flat," said the beat-up cat,
    "We're traveling boosters, you know."
Bud said, "Don't fear, you just wait here.
    It won't take me long to score."   40

Now Bud hesitated, 'cause he'd underrated
   And thought he could make a big sting.
But now he knew the shuck wouldn't do—
   He had to cop the real thing.

"You give me the dough, and I'll go score,"
   Said he, and then he was gone.
But he showed back quick, 'cause he was also sick,
   And they went to his pad to get on.

They pulled out two spikes, laid out two hypes,
   And rolled some one-dollar-bill gees.   50
They took some smack from a cellophane pack,
   And they both rolled up their sleeves.

"Go easy on it, 'cause it's high-percentage shit,"
   Said Bud. "So take it real slow.
A bag like this is so full of bliss
   It'll knock any old-time junkie to the floor."

The stud untied, the hipcat sighed,
   "Like, baby, I'm really high."
The stud made a pass and flashed a badge
   And said, "Dig, I'm the F.B.I."   60

The hipcat froze, then suddenly rose
   As if to make a grandstand.
Then he said, "What's the use? I've cooked my goose,"
   And gave himself up to the man.

They took him to jail and gave him no bail
   So he could slip away to the South.
And word of the bust, so grave and unjust,[1]
   Traveled from mouth to mouth.

---

[1]Bud's arrest was felt to be "unjust" not because Bud was innocent of the charge but because, as in the case of the narrator of "Kitty Barrett," it was based on illegal police entrapment. Line 54 of the sequel makes this point directly.

The numbers were all in, and there wasn't any skin;
    Crime was on a sudden decrease.   70
The ponies didn't peep, the dispatchers were asleep,
    And everyone was at peace.

The streets were at rest on the east and the west;
    The prowl cars weren't making a fuss.
Every hip stud had come to see Bud,
    And for hours there wasn't a bust.

The courtroom was full 'cause Bud had been pulled,
    And, truly like his name,
He never hollered but always followed
    The rules that went with the Game.   80

There were those who knew him, the agent who threw him,
    And those who just came to stare.
There was Whiskey-Top Ed, fucked up in the head
    And looking the worse for wear.

There was Fast-Fucking Annie, sitting on her fanny,
    Putting on airs like a queen,
Next to Long-Green Bill and Two-Bit Lil,
    Who had come just to be seen.

Long-Drawers Lucy was looking real juicy,
    And Sal the Dike was there.   90
Even Ann the Rabbit with the long dope habit
    Had managed to get the fare.

Big Ike from Chi was riding high
    Wearing a new sharkskin vine,
Leaning on his pillow while his number-one gorilla
    Was covering him well from behind.

Douche-Mouth Eddie with a pros named Betty
    Was calmly digging the scene,
When Phil the Fag showed up in drag
    On the arm of Smitty Cocaine.   100

Now when Bud came into court, voices fell short,
    And everyone strained to hear,
As D.A. Grace presented his case,
    And really went into high gear.

He said Bud wore a rich vine and had an
                   adding-machine mind
    And drove a Caddy as long as a train,
That he looked real square but was everywhere,
    A master of the long-shoe game.

The junkies all stared as they heard Bud's name smeared
    And drug all through the mud,   110
For Grace told in detail how Bud made the sale.
    It looked like the end for Bud.

Now J.P. Spence was the hipcat's defense,
    And known as an all-time great.
In his hand was Bud's two grand.
    Spence really held Bud's fate.

"I can't beat it," he said as he counted the bread.
    "The politicians just won't buy.
D.A. Grace has an airtight case,
    And you can't bribe the F.B.I.   120

"The D.A.'s scared and won't take no bread;
    The word's 'Hands off. No can do.'
Judge Stern is hot, and he's on the spot;
    So he'll make an example out of you."

Now the jury went out for a four-hour bout.
    The foreman was a plumber named Hodges.
He winked at Judge Stern and announced on return,
    "The Defendant is guilty on all charges."

The courtroom was still as a sudden hush fell,
    And Judge Stern cleared his throat.   130
"Have you anything to say before we send you away
    On the next Sing Sing boat?"

Bud said, "I'm not crying 'cause the D.A. was lying
    And left you with a notion.
He's an honest slob who's just doing his job.
    In fact, I hope the punk gets a promotion.

"I dug from the start you ain't got no heart
    When the narco flagged me down,
And I knew the report when I came into court,
    Like they knew it all over town.   140

"But I strayed from the code, and I copped a big load,
    And this is the price I must pay,
While all kinds of crime is raging full time
    All up and down Broadway.

"While some drunken villain rapes all of your children
    And pays a fine and goes free,
You sit on your ass like you got class
    And make a example out of me.

"Well, it's all the same, 'cause it's all in the Game,
    As I dug when I set out to play;   150
You got all the cards, and you fix the odds;
    And that's the price a poor dope fiend must pay."

"What you say is true," said Stern, looking blue,
    "But it's in the public eye.
You had your fun, but now you're done,
    'Cause I sentence you one to five."

THE RETURN OF HONKY-TONK BUD

If Honky-Tonk Bud's professional reputation is left somewhat uncertain in the toast that bears his name, there is no doubt of it in the sequel: he is a titan. The popularity which brought such luminaries as Big Ike from Chi and Cocaine Smitty to his trial in "Honky-Tonk Bud" is seen in "The Return" to represent real influence; so catastrophic was his arrest that the Supreme Court was forced to reverse his conviction.

Both the style and the plot of this poem differ so greatly from those of its predecessor that it is obvious they came from different sources; the first is humorous realism and the second facetious epic. But the character of Bud remains constant; he is as calm, deliberate, and competent in the extravagant sequel as in the earlier toast.

The references to Johnson (1. 58), U Thant (1. 59), Malcolm X (1. 63), and Khrushchev (1. 65) give us a fairly exact clue to the date, at least of this passage. Since Johnson took office in 1963 and Malcolm X died in 1964, the composition of these stanzas may safely be placed within a year of 1964.

Boxcar, who recited "The Return" almost without pausing to draw breath, had been a sort of runner in the Life; he did errands for the players, or so he said, in Jersey City. He had come to prison for some small crime committed on a visit to New York and was widening his circle of acquaintance. A black about twenty, he recited in a tense monotone as though fearful of forgetting a line, but his extensive repertoire made up for his lack of dramatic flair, and he was a welcome visitor to recreation-yard conversations. This version of "The Return of Honky-Tonk Bud," the only complete one encountered, was heard in 1966 in Auburn.

The Return of Honky-Tonk Bud

As the gate clanged shut and hit Bud in the butt,
    The Warden made this remark:
"For a cat so hip you sure made a slip.
    Tell me, where's your Cadillac parked?

"All your girls out in the free world
    Will forget that you're alive.
Yes, you're finished, friend, this is the end.
    So just be cool, and you might stay alive.

"In here you get beans and maggots steamed,
    Meatballs the size of a snail.   10
It's the best meal of the week; so don't you kick,
    Or we'll be feeding you slop in a pail.

"Those real boss meals are eaten by wheels,
    Nobles and all of that jazz.
Well, forget it, chump, you must be drunk;
    Your good-doing days are in the past.

"In here you're kept low, just so's you'll know
    Who's boss of your new home.
If you think this is bluff, just start some stuff,
    And we'll break you out a new tombstone.   20

"We'll blister your rump with a young tree stump
    From your head to the soles of your feet;
And if you open your mouth just once to shout,
    We'll beat all the gold out your teeth.

"Now I don't doubt one day you'll get out,
    But just when the judge didn't say;
And if I know Brooklyn, with the shape you're in,
    You're here for a real stay.

"So pick up your plate, line up and wait,
    And don't grumble when the beans pass your nose.   30
Just resign yourself to eat it or else—
    You know how the rest of it goes."

Bud slowly spinned with a sly old grin,
    As only he knew how.
He picked up his fork and started to walk
    Towards the messhall to cop his chow.

On his face Bud was beaming, but his mind was scheming
    How to give Judge Stern back his time.
Bud wasn't scared, 'cause there was nothing he feared
    Except maybe losing his mind.   40

Late that night he scribed a kite
    To five different parts of the world.
Four went to men and a limp-wrist friend,
    And the fifth went to his main girl.

He didn't have ink, so he stopped the sink,
    Cut his finger and wrote with his blood.
And so they'd be hip to who wrote the scrip,
    He endorsed them "The Hipcat Stud."

The first letter went whence he copped his hemp—
    Red China—Mao Tse-tung.
The letter read thus: "Don't kick up no fuss;
    Just spread the word to the tong.

"They got me up tight, and you know that ain't right.
    In fact, they even flagged me wrong.[1]
Don't send the troops out, just send the girl scouts,
    'Cause they alone total eighty million strong.

[1]See the note to l. 67 in "Honkey-Tonk Bud," p. 56.

"I've written to Lyndon, and if he will listen,
    I'm sure that he'll come in.
And if he can't, my main man U Thant
    Will have to shake up the U.N.   60

"Yes, I wrote him, too, and, between me and you,
    I think he can handle my case.
If I'd thought it was best, I'd have wrote Malcolm X,
    But this isn't a matter of race.

"I also wrote Nikita, who's down in Cubarita,
    But I think he'd cause too much harm,
'Cause he's a fool who knows no rule,
    And he just might drop that bomb.

"I've made an appeal about my raw deal,
    But the shysters keep crying for bread.   70
If the courts don't soon wake, it may be too late:
    The whole hemisphere might wake up dead.

"Because Khrushchev ain't jiving, he's bad as a lion,
    And the stink from my trial you can smell.
He's one mad Russian who may just push the button
    That will blow us all straight to hell."

That night Bud slept hard with a heavy heart,
    And his mind was filled to the brim
With way-out dreams and legal schemes,
    'Cause his future was looking real dim.   80

He dreamed of the day he first started to play
    In the game of life called Power.
He saw in his mind the place and the time,
    And he even remembered the hour.

Bud was only a kid when he first made his bid
    For a piece of the spoiler's due,
And with his haul he established a stall,
    And from then on he really flew.

He started his climb with one thin dime
 Where the Mexicana Rose got her start.   90
But that's another story and much too gory;
 In fact, it would break your heart.

Bud went on strong from that day on
 To climb to the heights of the Game.
In his spare time he refined his mind
 And went on to fortune and fame.

Bud's dreams took him back to Hackensack,
 To a section called Hanging Rope.
It was here by chance that he found romance
 In the pleasures men find in dope.   100

It was a ship's port where he met the old sport,
 A descendant of Jean Lafitte.
He had circled the globe forty times or more
 And owned twenty ships in his fleet.

They called him "King Neptune," and he made quite
     a fortune
 Running guns in the First World War.
He played host to those who paid the most,
 And you'd be surprised at the action he saw.

From both friends and foes he accepted kilos
 Of narcotics, as payment and gratis,   110
And down through the years he stood without peers
 In his role of kingpin status.

He took a shine to Bud, the Hipcat Stud,
 'Cause Bud was mentally free.
Just to see what he'd do, he gave Bud two
 And was convinced when he came back with three.

He said, "Son, I'm getting on,
    And I'm looking for someone to fill my shoes."
Bud said, "It's true you're getting old, and I'll play
        the rôle,
    But spare me those dying blues."   120

This made Neptune smile, and after a while
    He told Bud the things he would do.
"I've got enough cocaine to put Fort Knox to shame,
    And I'm giving it all to you.

"I've been bringing in junk by the steamer trunk;
    The narcos never laid a hand on me.
It was the people I knew and the things they'd do:
    For twenty years I've had diplomatic immunity.

"My only flag, of which I still brag,
    Was the Roger flying high on my deck;   130
Through enemy lines congested with mines
    I've sailed and gotten respect.

"I once rode out a storm around Cape Horn
    When a typhoon ran up my back.
I lost all my crew and my Chinese cook too,
    But my cargo was all intact.

"The four wild winds were my best friends,
    Whirlpools and icebergs my guides.
I took Byrd to the Pole and showed him the scroll
    That taught the Navy how to measure the tides."   140

Bud laughed till he cried, but the look in his eyes
    Told a story that was void of mirth.
He knew this was no act, 'cause the old man dealt
        in fact,
    And there was no telling what the man was worth.

The very same day, Neptune passed away,
    And before the town heard he was dead,
The coroner got a bill and the lawyers had the will,
    And this is the way it read:

"To Honky-Tonk Bud, the Hipcat Stud,
    I bequeath everything I own,   150
From the shoes on my feet and my whole ship fleet
    To the treasure I've buried in Nome.

"Give him my maps with their location facts
    And the keys to my castles in Spain.
And then let him try all that money can buy
    From aspirin to Lady Cocaine.

"Give him the keys to the vault where I keep the bulk
    Of the fortune I keep in store.
Let him try on my rings, my diamonds and things,
    And if he wants them, buy him some more."   160

Beyond any doubt this knocked Bud out:
    To be heir to a tax-free fortune.
For him it was rare, but he said a prayer
    And silently thanked old Neptune.

Bud smiled when he heard the lawyer's next word,
    As the reading of the will continued:
"Keep your health and spend all this wealth,
    'Cause you sho-nuff can't take it with you."

Bud woke with a start when he heard the guard
    As he came with the morning mail.   170
Would his hopes come true and mail go through,
    Or would his efforts fail?

Before Bud copped, the police stopped
    To censor what the telegram said.
It read so tough and was saying so much
    That the hack fell over dead.

The paper hit the ground when the screw fell down,
    Lying out in all his array.
Bud screamed and jumped. "Come get this chump
    And tell me what my telegram say."   180

Just beyond the door, lying on the floor,
    Was the cable as bright as could be.
Bud measured the span by the reach of his hand,
    But the space was too far, he could see.

His heart skipped a beat as he pictured defeat.
    If only there was some string, he could fetch it.
It didn't look good from where he stood.
    Man, what was in that message?

His eyes searched the room and fell on the broom,
    But that missed by a yard.   190
His plight was sad, and that made him mad,
    And his efforts became twice as hard.

He looked at the cable, though he wasn't quite able
    To distinguish the print on the script.
But there's no sense in crying, he had to keep trying,
    'Cause it just might be the writ.

"It's too long for a check, but what the heck,
    Still that's just a guess.
I'd feel much better if I could get the letter,
    And the hell with the rest of the mess."   200

"It's a Dear John mark," said a voice from the dark,
    "Somebody done split with your wife."
Bud said, "If the doors were open, I'd know who'd spoken,
    And my razor would split with your life.

"You're probably one of those chumps with the
                southern mumps
    All over the top of your head.
Maybe you don't know, but I'd lay you low
    For the things your mouth just said."

In a voice that wavered an old-timer quavered,
    "That's Honky-Tonk, the Hipcat Stud,   210
So cool it, baby, and don't act crazy;
    It's plain you ain't hip to Bud.

"He needs some rope, and you better hope
    That he cops with a little bit of luck.
If the news ain't right, you'll be up tight
    When these cell doors open up."

The noise went dead as this was said,
    And they heard him rip his linen.
He fished the cable and was sitting at his table.
    The contents had him grinning.   220

It was a report from the Supreme Court
    And was signed by the highest of judges.
It was two pages long and read like a song,
    And Honky-Tonk started packing his luggage.

Bud re-read the lines two more times,
    And the message was just too sweet:
There was a revision, and the judges' decision
    Was putting Bud back on the street.

"It came through, fellows; so tell my mellows
    I'll spring 'em, 'cause I've got the price."   230
A con in Five Cell by the name of Dell
    Said, "Dig it, ain't he nice!"

"My dear hip friend," the letter began,
      "Here's some splow and a big shoddy-doo.
I know that cell was natural hell."
      (Bud muttered, "All that's true.")

"I must confess I'll straighten this mess,
      And I know just how you must feel.
But we got proof that justice goofed
      When she rendered your raw deal.   240

"She rigged her scales to put you in jail
      For things you did not do.
It depresses me and sets you free,
      'Cause they railroaded you.

"Yes, your main man, Dapper Dan,
      Appealed to the crowd on the set.
His rap was boss and really got across
      When they saw that his eyes were wet.

"He got to their minds when he wrinkled his vines;
      This act alone shook their heads;   250
It was no joke the words Dan spoke,
      'Cause they knew how he felt about his threads.

"And your lady friend, she sure came in,
      Like all thoroughbreds will do;
She wrote the girls around the world
      And told them what happened to you.

"She sent a kite to every girl of the night,
      From Egyptian to Eskimo.
Some sent mules and others jewels,
      But all of them sent some dough.   260

"I wasn't surprised at the way she connived.
      Day and night she played her hand.
   And if she was asked what was her task,
      She answered, 'To free my man.'

"Even the junkies gave up their monkeys,
 'Cause the pushers started something that was tough;
They all got down with the addicts in town
 And donated a million bucks worth of stuff.

"Two-Gun Green was on the scene,
 And also Pimping Sam;   270
Green wore his guns and Sam brought two nuns,
 And they donated fourteen grand.

"Some rookie dude made a move
 And shot Green down in blood:
But before he died he caught my eye
 And said, 'Get this dough to Bud.'

"A new crime release broke the peace,
 There were riots in all five boroughs.
The National Guard were called for the job,
 But they couldn't erase the trouble.   280

"The State Police patroled the street;
 They enforced the F.B.I. plan.
Somebody offed Pagent the narco agent,
 But they never found the man.

"D.A. Grace got shot in the face;
 A bomb was found in his short.
And Richard D. Spence hasn't been seen since
 That fateful day in court.

"But I got a wire he got caught in a fire
 And that his ashes were hot and fiery,   290
That when his family came for his remains,
 They couldn't find enough to bury.

"The World's Fair went busted, no one could be trusted,
 The U.N. burned to the ground;
Congress was affected, a new Cabinet elected,
 The White House was turned all around.

"Bud, all this is true that I'm telling you,
   These are the highlights of the tale.
Now I'm scared for me, so I'm setting you free,
   And I'm ready from now on to go your bail.   300

"As a Supreme Court judge I wouldn't budge,
   If the judicial laws didn't waver.
   But I want to be around to enjoy this town,
   So of course I had to rule in your favor."

With grip in hand, Bud called the man,
   "Roll 'em, Cap, and don't be slow.
I got the word, or haven't you heard?
   Hurry up and open my door."

The hacks got to fumbling, running and stumbling,
   Everybody asking everybody else.   310
The way they were calling, bumping heads and falling,
   You'd think Bud was God himself.

The Warden came in with some official friend.
   You could tell that the man had class;
He wore the same type of clothes that the Warden wore,
   But his shoulders were covered with brass.

They escorted Bud out, and there is no doubt
   That here another story begins.
But I'm tired and beat, and I got to get some sleep.
   So here's where this story ends.   320

P.S.,my friend, before I end,
   Let me remind you, though I hate to boast:
When someone asks you who wrote this trash,
   Just say Upsetter and J.J. wrote this toast.

GOOD-DOING WHEELER

The victim-heroes of "Kitty Barrett" and "Honky-Tonk Bud" went to prison because they were outsmarted by the police, but disaster springs from other sources in toasts. Wheeler, here, falls because his best friend sells him out for a bottle of cheap wine. A pathetic and credible little anecdote, "Good-Doing Wheeler" is one of the most structurally ingenious in the collection. When well performed, it always brings great surprise and amusement to first-time hearers.

The absence of resentment at Joe's betrayal (11. 39–40) gives us some idea of the resignation with which such things are taken in the Life; the attempted theft of a friend's woman in "Sugar Hill" is a much greater offense against its code.

Wheeler was not a particularly heroic figure even in his good-doing days. His chief accomplishment seems to have been the acquisition of a wardrobe which must surely stand alone in the annals of the mack.

On Christmas 1955, a group was sitting around one of the oil-drum stoves in the yard of Clinton Prison in Dannemora, telling toasts. A couple of young blacks made false starts with "Good-Doing Wheeler," but everyone kept interrupting with corrections until Superjunkie spoke up with the version given here. Superjunkie was a dashing, light-skinned black from New Orleans who had been involved with narcotics since the 40's, before it became fashionable, and as one of the rare old-time junkies he had a certain authority. His nickname, like those of most prison inmates, was ironic; it referred to his grandiose tales of his own prowess in acquiring, using, and selling narcotics. Nobody, including himself, took these stories very seriously, and he would cheerfully back down from any challenge to his veracity. His stock of toasts was large—learned, he said, back in New Orleans. All of them were about drugs.

Good-Doing Wheeler

Good-Doing Wheeler, the big-time dope dealer
    Came from up on Boston Road.[1]
You never seen a man so clean;
    His clothes was atomically sewed.

The ties he wore didn't come from no store;
    They were knitted with meticulous care.
His socks were boss, and, man, did they cost!
    For they were woven of a young girl's hair.

His handkerchieves were the envy of thieves;   10
    He had them made by hand.
And his fabulous sky was broke so fly
    That the city had it banned.

His shoes were thin, like baby 'gator skin,
    Yet he wore each pair but once.
They looked like suede, and dig how they was made—
    From the hair of virgin cunts.

His topnotch socks were made from the locks
    of choice young girls' hair;
Yet he threw them away three times a day
    And switched to another pair.   20

Of his underclothes no one knows;
    Curiosity has caused some to die.
They were delivered in a short built like a fort
    And guarded by the F.B.I.

I forgot to mention how he paid attention
    To his shirts, but you'd think it's a lie;
The son-of-a-bitch wouldn't wear a stitch
    If it weighed more than a sigh.

His white-on-whites were made from lights
    With a touch of helium gas,   30
And Christian Dior was designing more
    Of pure dew and woven grass.

Now it was a known fact, if you wanted some smack,
    Good-Doing always had.
But the rollers got wise, which was no surprise,
    And decided to shake down his pad.

Wheeler's main man Joe was an old wino,
    And from here on things get grim;
A narco cop pulled Joe drop by drop
    And got the keys off of him.   40

Wheeler denied and even cried.
    He said the whole thing was a frame.
But now he was hooked, his goose was cooked,
    With 1751 next to his name.[2]

Wheeler's mistake, as he learned too late,
    Was not being hip to the latest word.
Too late to pray, he cursed the day
    That Gallo made Thunderbird.[3]

At his trial he lied a while,
    But even he could see the end.   50
So he copped out to Subdivision Two,[4]
    And the judge said five to ten.

[1] A street in a black neighborhood of the Bronx.

[2] Section 1751 of the Penal Law of New York defines "Violations of the Public Health Law with respect to narcotic drugs" and establishes the punishment for "any person who shall ... sell ... any narcotic drug" (*McKinney's Consolidated Laws of New York Annotated* [1967], Vol. XXXIX, p. 585).

[3] Thunderbird wine was first offered for sale by Gallo Wineries in 1956 and quickly established itself at sixty cents a quart as a favorite of alcoholics. Indeed a password exchanged between two of them went, "What's the word?" "Thunderbird." "What's the price?" "Thirty twice." "Where'd you cop?" "Liquor shop."

[4] Subdivision Two of Section 1751 defines the lesser charge of possessing "any narcotic drug ... with intent to ... sell ... the same or any part thereof" (*McKinney's*, Vol. XXXIX, p. 585).

Now five to ten is enough, my friend,
    To cramp anybody's style.
And with five from the start Wheeler blew his heart,
    His broad, bankroll, and smile.

Well, he did three-four and they showed him the door.[5]
    It sure felt great to be free.
When he got to the city it looked mighty pretty,
    And he decided to go on a spree.   60

He thought of his dough, which was getting low,
    As back on the streets he came,
But he swore up and down all over the town
    That he was through with the Game.

He said, "I won't wink at an occasional drink
    Or even a stick of pot.
But as for stuff, I've had enough—
    Four years ago was my last shot.

"I'm going to find Pearl; you know that old girl.
    I know she'll see me straight."   70
But everyone knew Good-Doing had blew.
    He was three years four months too late.

Now everyone pinned as Good-Doing moved in,
    To see when him and his woman met,
'Cause since he'd been gone she'd come on strong
    And was one of the swingingest broads on the set.

No one could know how things would go,
    For he once had her up tight.
Like all the rest, this was the test
    Of how he stood when his pockets was light.   80

[5]Three years and four months, two-thirds of a minimum sentence of five years, is the statutory period which must be served before applying for release on parole in New York state.

He saw her in back of a chicken shack
    Holding a trick by the hand.
She fluttered her eye, brushed his fly,
    And beat his back slide for a grand.

Well, it wasn't far to get back to the bar,
    And Good-Doing watched without a blink.
She giggled, "Oh, honey, your jokes are so funny.
    Let's have just one more drink."

When the trick raised his glass, that was his ass,
    As his slid to his knees from the bar.   90
She gave the eye to a bouncer nearby,
    Who carried him out to the car.

She wheeled real quick, sizing up another trick,
    And Wheeler said, "Bless my soul!
If it isn't Pearl, my old girl!
    Barkeep, let the good times roll."

He felt like a fool, but he grabbed a stool
    And came on real assured.
He flashed a smile in his old-time style
    And said, "Baby, what's the word?   100

"I understood you was doing good,
    And, momma, you sure look fine.
From now on it'll be just you and me.
    Everything will be like old times."

Pearl turned around with a great big frown
    And looked Wheeler dead in his eyes.
She said, "Word got around you was back in town,
    But I thought you'd got wise.

"Now listen, honey, if you're spending money,
    That's perfectly all right with me.   110
But I've got to know just how long is your dough,
    And I don't want to hear; I want to see.

"I don't go for no flash, I'm out for cash,
    And the bigger the bucks the better.
If you've got short dough, just let me know.
    The rest you can write in a letter.

"You once had me up tight when things were all right,
    And you had your Fleetwood Caddy.
You were fly enough with your vines and stuff
    To be my loving daddy.   120

"But times have changed. I'm out of your range.
    I'm down, sweet-loving, and swift.
For the Pearl you once knew the whole world has blew;
    I wouldn't have the bitch back as a gift.

"Now there you sit talking that fairy-tale shit.
    You must be the world's biggest lame.
So get in the wind, go where you been.
    Cop and blow is part of the game.

"Don't stand and stare, for it'll get you nowhere.
    I know you think I'm just a dirty whore.   130
But so's your mother and your faggot-ass brother."
    Then she rounded and stepped out the door.

There was a total hush, for Good-Doing was crushed,
    And the bartender said, "I don't want trouble.
I don't mean to be funny, but I'm here to make money,
    And you ordered the whole house a double."

So Good-Doing paid the tab and took a cab
    To a Hundred and Sixteenth Street,
Where he tried to blow the rest of his dough
    But ended up getting beat.   140

From that day on, Good-Doing was gone,
   And his vines went one by one.
He once paid his dues by selling his shoes
   For some sneakers and a three-dollar gun.[6]

He developed the habit of living like a rabbit,
   Running from hole to hole.
Once you'd cop, up he would pop.
   Have Gun, Will Travel was his rôle.

Now he's known as Greasy Wheeler, the boss ham stealer,[7] 150
   Trying to make it the best way he can.
But being real greasy, it ain't very easy,
   Dodging the P.O *and* the man.

Well, I guess by now you've figured somehow
   That Greasy Wheeler is me.
I've come down front 'cause there's something I want;
   And I've earned it, don't you agree?

Now I've got a gig, and it's going to be big,
   But keep it under your hat.
I mean it to be just you and me—   160
   I'm sure you know where I'm at.

You know, it's a drag; I copped a bad bag,
   And, Jim, lately things have been rotten.
But when I make that big sting, I'll straighten you
                              first thing,
   If you'll save me a little on the cotton.[8]

---

[6]Sneakers are the badge of the burglar, a relatively low-status figure in the Life.

[7]Ham stealing: stealing just to eat, rather than for profit. A ham stealer is thus the lowest-status player in the Life.

[8]A common request by unprovided addicts for such traces of heroin as remain on the cotton with which their luckier friends have prepared the narcotic. When heroin is *cooked up* (dissolved in water for injection), it is then drawn up from the spoon or bottle cap into a wad of cotton to prevent contact between the needle and the metal container, to avoid losing any of the drug, and to filter the solution. See "King Heroin II," 1. 25.

THE FALL

Singled out by Labov (1968:61) as exemplifying toasts "at their highest level," this is one of the best developed pieces in the literature. Indeed, the rhetorical elegance of its opening stanzas seems almost excessive for a folk poem. The ingenuity of its language, the smoothness of its narrative flow, and the professionalism of its prosody all bear suspicious marks of sophistication. But the ring of authenticity can be heard clearly not only in the language but in the story itself: "The Fall" is a tale paralleled by many falls in the Life.

Doe Eye held an audience spellbound on a gallery in Attica with this narrative one evening in 1963.

The Fall

Now some of you guys might be surprised
    At what I'm about to say,
And say, "Who is this lame who says he knows the Game,
    And where did he learn to play?"

Well, I'd like to tell of how I fell
    And the trick fate played on me;
So gather around, and I'll run it down
    And unravel my pedigree.

It was Saturday night, and the jungle was bright,
    And the Game was stalking its prey.   10
The code was crime in the neon line,
    And the weak were doomed to pay.

When crime begun, when daughter fought son,
    And your dad, he lay in jail,
As your mom lay awoke with her heart almost broke
    'Cause the pad was up for sale;

Where blood was shed for the sake of bread,
    And drunks rolled for their poke
By the sleight-of-hand of a Murphy man
    Or the words that a con man spoke;   20

Where addicts prowl with a tigerish scowl
    In search of that lethal blow,
And the wino cringes from the canned-heat binges
    And finds his grave in the snow;

Where belles of vice sell love for a price,
    And even the law is corrupt,
As you go down trying, you keep on crying,
    "Man, it's a bitter cup!"

Where the jungle creed says the strong must feed
    On any prey at hand,   30
I was branded a beast and sat at the feast
    Before I was a man.

In the gaudy display of the midnight ray
    Lit up like a Christmas toy,
I made my play for a female prey
    At the time I was just a boy.

I was young and prancy, and pot was my fancy;
    I was known as the adequate male.
But I curse the day I made my play
    For that sidewalk Jezebel.   40

She was a brown-skin moll like a Chinese doll,
    Walking up and down in sin.
Back and forth she'd trod with a wink and a nod
    To the nearest whorehouse den.

Now it wasn't by chance that I caught her glance,
    'Cause I intended to steal this dame;
So I smiled with glee and said, "Golly gee,
    It's time for the kid to game."

Her eyes shone bright in the neon light,
 And from them a teardrop fell.   50
When I asked her why, she began to cry
 And tell me this bitter tale

About some guy who blacks her eye
 And takes all the dough she gets,
And how she lays in jail, and he won't go her bail
 And dares her to call it quits.

So I said, "Bitch, dry your tears and have no fears,
 For the kind lover is here.
And I'm staking my claim for a piece of this game
 And vowing I'll have no peer."   60

Jim, the bitch looked at me like a slave set free,
 And said, "Then I'm your girl."
And her man didn't stir as I split with her,
 And we made it all over the world.

She caught on fast as the months rolled past,
 She played it to the bitter end,
And a better whore I've yet to know,
 Although a dog is man's best friend.

She was a three-way wench, played Jasper in a pinch,
 And took 'em around the horn.   70
No Jean or John this whore couldn't con,
 'Cause that trick was never born.

She was a good shot broad and a pro at fraud,
 And drag she played like a vet.
She played stuff like an ace, never lost a case,
 And put many a mark in debt.

She ranked with the best in the East and the West
 When her boosting hand came down.
She'd steal knots out of knees and Fido's fleas;
 She'd steal out many a town.   80

Now I've heard whores cry 'bout the wind being high
    And the law being on their tail,
About snow and sleet being asshole deep,
    And the tricks can go to hell.

In a greasy spoon or a juke saloon,
    You can find them killing their time,
Crying hard-luck tears and sucking up beers,
    And the pimps ain't getting a dime.

Turning half-dollar tricks to make a fix,
    With the pussy doing the pimping—   90
They're just ruining the name of a hell of a game,
    'Cause the pimps are doing the simping.

Now they're ducking and hiding, slipping and sliding,
    Sucking them party packs,
And nodding so tough from fucking with stuff
    Till the bitch can't see her tracks.

Monday morning for sure you can't find the whore,
    'Cause some rookie cop has caught her,
And you pawn your shit to get her a writ,
    And the bitch ain't made a quarter.   100

About a month or two, when the rent's overdue,
    And the landlord's hopping mad,
She slides 'tween your sheets with no night receipts,
    Saying, "Daddy, the night was bad."

Why, you could cop her lid for the lowest bid,
    You could set her ass on fire;
You could dig in her cunt for a solid month,
    'Cause she's the cheapest whore you can hire.

But you know the price when you deal in vice,
    You know it's a steady grind;   110
And a bitch has to go and be a real good whore
    To beat this triple bitch of mine.

She dropped many a bug on many a mug
  Too numerous to call their name;
Many a sap got caught in her trap
  By the lure they call the Game.

For a lick and lap from her mellow cap
  The tricks would fight a duel;
Why, all the long bread was made with her head—
  This bitch was a real jewel.   120

She had a good round-eye, and that's no lie;
  How the trickhouse door would swing!
Many a nut got busted in her butt,
  For the rag didn't mean a thing.

Anywhere she'd follow the righteous dollar,
  To hell if she had to go,
And be there waiting to trick with old Satan—
  Man, I had me a money-making whore.

Like a sex machine she would walk between
  Raindrops, snow, and hail,   130
And stand on hot bricks to lure the tricks,
  Come cyclone, blizzard, or gale.

She tricked with Frenchmen, torpedoes, and henchmen;
  To her it was all the same.
With Japs and Jews, Apaches and Sioux,
  And breeds I cannot name;

With Chinks and Greeks, with Arabs and freaks;
  She tricked in the House of God.
No son-of-a-gun would this whore shun
  Who could pay to use his rod.   140

Why, the sun didn't set when her cunt wasn't wet
  And her pockets heavy with gold.
And many a trick with a weekend dick
  Got took for his entire roll.

Now I laid and played off the dough she made
    From the coast to old Broadway;
My game was strong 'cause my money was long.
    I made this business pay.

But the trouble began when I ranked my hand
    And stopped blowing and started to hit.   150
Why, Jim, you know, I blew that dough
    Faster than any one whore could get.

Then I blew my shack, my Cadillac,
    My rug up off the floor.
I sold my ice at a pawnshop price
    And shot up all that dough.

I stole from Ma, I swindled Pa;
    I sold my pedigreed pup.
I pawned my threads, sold my bed,
    And shot my TV up.   160

My woman cried and damn near died
    When I went off with her mink.
But I stayed in my rôle and stole and sold
    Everything but the kitchen sink.

Now my deadliest blow came when the whore
    Took sick and couldn't gin.
The Chinaman spoke, and it wasn't a joke,[1]
    For I knew this was the end.

She had bleeding piles and inflamed bile;
    For a month she couldn't pee.   170
I was shot to hell when her ovaries fell,
    And things looked bad for me.

---

[1]Labov et al. (1968:65) mention these obscure references to "the Chinaman" as defeating their efforts at identification and say that he "appears here as a symbol of death and fate." A less resounding but perhaps more probable explanation might be merely that the Chinaman was the source of narcotics and that he "spoke" or "took his toll" when someone needed his services.

But believe me, friend, when lockjaw set in,
  The Chinaman took his toll.[2]
Her head was dead, her ass was lead,
  The lips of her cunt was cold.

So down I fell to the depths of hell,
  For I'd put myself in the cross.
As my habit grew tall, my money grew small;
  Everything I had was lost.   180

But I wanted to be fair and on the square,
  I didn't want to buck the saw;
So I said what the hell, since this bitch ain't well,
  I'll get her a wife-in-law.

I said, "Lay on there till you're feeling fair
  And can get back in the street,
While I do my best to convalesce
  And get back on my feet.

"There's that cute little bitch with the whorehouse itch
  That I could latch onto,   190
And that red-headed whore who's rearing to go
  If the deal's okay with you.

"There ain't a bitch in the Game with your kind of name
  For kicking the mud you kick.
So you lay on there till you're feeling fair,
  And we'll see can we make them click."

Now a bitch like this is a good man's bliss;
  She had everything it took.
But she had one fault—when she was caught,
  The bitch couldn't lose the hook.   200

[2]Ibid.

"Hell no," she said, "I'll see you dead
    Before I'll let you go.
The black coach of sorrow will pick up your
                  ass tomorrow[3]
    If you step beyond that door.

"I blew my health in a bid for wealth,
    So you could play your bit.
But you went hophead and blew the bread;
    Now you're talking that stable shit.

I'm not going for no brush or no bum whore's rush,
    And I know that's what you plan,   210
Talking all slick with all that bullshit—
    Motherfucker, you ain't no man.

I'm hip to the way you pimps try to play
    And the lugs you drop on a frail;
But if this shit don't cease, I'll call the police
    And bury your ass in jail."

I packed my shit, firing to split,
    And this is what I said:
"If that's the way you want to play,
    Go make your own damn bread.   220

"Bitch, you ain't no lame, you know the Game;
    They call it cop and blow.
You've had your run, and now you're done.
    I need me another whore.

"I can't cop no swag with no swayback nag
    Whose thoroughbred days are past.
I'd look pretty damn silly putting a cripple-ass filly
    On a track that's much too fast.

---

[3]Labov (ibid., 59) has "black *coats* of sorrow" in this line, but the allusion is evidently to a hearse. The pronunciation often allows either reading.

"I was going to put you in charge of a trickhouse lodge
  And give you some girls to rule;   230
But you spoke of hell and sending me to jail—
  Bitch, you must be a goddam fool.

" 'Cause a bitch can't shit without a good man's wit,
  And one monkey don't stop no show.
Why, in a hour or two I'll have me a slew
  Of bitches out there to whore.

"So step aside, 'cause I'm fixing to slide—
  I mean get the fuck off my back.
'Cause my money's low, and I need me a whore
  Who can run that speedy track."   240

While laying back in another whore's shack,
  About to make my plea,
I heard a thunder that the door shook under
  And wondered what the fuck it could be.

A roller walked in; on his face was a grin
  Mined with a deadly expression.
He said, "If you're Bud, the pimping stud,
  All I want is a signed confession."

My woman stood there with her finger in the air.
  "That's him," she cried with glee.   250
"That's the son-of-a-bitch with the con man pitch
  Who made a whore out of me."

A crashing blow sent me to the floor;
  I sank in a black repose.
When I awoke, my nose was broke,
  And blood all over my clothes.

I played it strong, but it wasn't long
  Before they took me to court.
You should have seen the shit that bitch had writ
  In the books of the police report.   260

Which just goes to show that the strongest whore
    Can give in to that female simping.
This bitch was born with a female scorn
    That got me two counts of pimping.

Now here I lay in jail in a six-by-six cell,
    Watching the sun rise in the East.
As the mornings chill the jungle still
    I think of that slumbering beast.

Farewell to the night, to the neon light,
    Farewell to you one and all.   270
And farewell to the Game; may it still be the same
    When I get done doing this fall.

DUMBO THE JUNKIE

Not all toasts are about epic heroes like Honky-Tonk Bud or even sometimes successful men like Long-Shoe Sam, Good-Doing Wheeler, and Duriella's pimp; some toasts are clearly stories of failure from the beginning. Dumbo has had better days, of course, but we do not hear of them. This story of a woman's desertion deals only with the misery of its hero.

Like Duriella, Kitty Barrett, and the "brown-skin moll like a Chinese doll" who brought the hero of "The Fall" down, Dumbo's girl is judged by white standards; her skin is like peanut butter, as Duriella's is like copper, and her hair, if not blonde, is at least long and wavy. Dumbo's despair at her loss seems based on sincere feeling for her, and he thus joins the narrator of "Duriella" as a romantic.

Recited by Duke in Auburn, 1964.

Dumbo the Junkie

I was sitting in the Dewdrop Inn, drinking pink
champagne,
When in walked Dumbo the junkie, dripping wet from
the rain.

He was wearing an antique raglan and a fucked-up hat
As he strolled over to the table where me and my girl
was at.

His shoes were worn, and his vine was beat,
And he hardly had strength enough to pull up a seat.

"Dumbo, my man," I said, "have a meal on me.
You ain't eaten lately, it's plain to see."

He said, "A meal I need, that much is true,
But I'd rather you'd loan me a dollar or two."   10

"Here's a pound, Dumbo, don't pay me back,
For I dug you were sick and needed some smack.

"I can see that you're doing real bad.
Whatever happened to all of that money you had?"

He said, "Well, being as you're my friend,
I'll run you down my story from beginning to end.

"It started in a town a bit down the way
Where I had to chop cotton to earn my pay.

"I'd say it was about ten years ago
When I met a hustler by the name of Joe.   20

"He went for me in a great big way
And taught me how to hustle for a year and a day.

"After I'd hustled a dollar or two,
He taught me all the tricks he knew.

"Then I met this choice chick, fresh out of school,
Sweet nineteen, a virgin and a fool.

"Her name was Yvette, and it fitted her to a T.
After our first conversation, she went for me.

"She had peanut butter skin and long wavy hair,
And the limbs she had were really a pair.   30

"Her breasts were full, she had great big thighs,
A cute little nose and freakish eyes.

"She had a topnotch education, boss as could be,
So it didn't take long to teach her what Joey taught me.

"She loved to shoot dope and have a real good time,
Till soon her habit was longer than mine.

"I bought her clothes and gave her dough
Till I found out she planned to run off with Joe.

"I cried on my bed for an hour and a half;
I even read a comic book, but I still couldn't laugh.   40

"So I shot an eighth of shit and went back to bed,
Figuring by morning I'd surely be dead.

"Well, as you can see, I must have pulled through,
Or I wouldn't be sitting here rapping to you.

"I woke up next morning with a broken heart
And figured I'd snuff Joey and get a new start.

"Well, as you may know, Joey is dead.
It was me caught him behind and shot him through
                          the head.

"The police couldn't hold me, for they had no proof,
And when Yvette heard the news, she jumped off the roof. 50

"Well, ever since then I've been doing real bad,
And that's what happened to every dime I had."

And with tears in his eyes and a heart full of pain,
Dumbo picked up his hat and walked back in the rain.

SUGAR HILL

One of the few really moralistic pieces among the toasts, "Sugar Hill" is reminiscent of the broadside ballads hawked at murderers' executions in 18th-century England. Though "The Signifying Monkey II," "Kitty Barrett," and the preceptive toasts contain notes of practical advice, "Sugar Hill" is alone here in ending on a note of moral warning based on personal confession. The crimes of other narrators are reported with triumph, but the narrator of this toast has done something more serious than breaking the law. The Thoroughbred Kid from Sugar Hill has violated the moral code of the Life: he has "crossed a pal."

In "Dumbo the Junkie" it is not stated whether Joe deliberately set out to steal the hero's woman—and consequently his livelihood—but Dumbo calmly reports having "snuffed" him anyway. The Thoroughbred Kid is luckier and survives, but his moral position is the same as Joe's, and he clearly accepts the fact. The note of contrition he sounds (11. 29–32, 39) is as rarely heard in toasts as it is in the Life.

Duke, who recited this in Auburn in 1964, considered it one of the oldest toasts he knew. He said that he had learned it from an old player on the West Coast in the late 1950's but that it came from the 30's or earlier. Both the tone and the theme of the toast seem to confirm the statement.

Sugar Hill

The rest was a bullshit story, but this is no
                                    fairy tale;
I'm now about to tell you why I really came to jail.

I thought I'd like to travel, to get a taste of life,
So I stole a car in Harlem and split New York that night.

My first stop was in Philly; I took the town by surprise.
I pulled off a couple of pretty good stings and laid
        low to avoid the eyes.

I stayed in a beat-up rooming house, the poorest of the lot,
But where all the hippest people stayed when they didn't
        want to get caught.

It was there I met a whore named Tina, a foxy kind
        of doll,
Dope Fiend Willy, Ed the Con Man, and a little punk
        named Sol.   10

Frankie the Pimp had a room there, and so did four of
        his whores.
Dolores the Booster lived in style with her zanzy
        roommate Rose.

Now Rose was a chick who stood five-six and had a body
        much in demand.
She told me she blew in from Frisco and was looking for
        a man.

So I ran down a game to her that would trick the
        slickest of whores,
And by nightfall I'd pulled her, and she decided
        to pack her clothes.

The first place we stopped was Chicago, which both of
        us seemed to like,
And while hanging around the Blue Note, I met a pimp
        named Ike.

He had a choice chick named Dolly, a standout among
        the whores,
Who'd bought Ike a powder-blue Coupe de Ville and   20
        a lot of pretty clothes.

We all hung out together while the girls brought in
                    the dough,
And I knew I had it made there within a month or so.

Things were looking pretty juicy, and I didn't have
                    a care
As I slipped into the lounge one night to have
                    a couple there.

While sitting in the barroom digging a crazy sound,
I heard my first name spoken, and so I turned around.

I saw Ike's girl before me. She said she had lots
                    of dough
And that if we went away together, no one would need
                    to know.

Now I'd never crossed a pal before and never been on
                    the run;
Yet I slipped into my pad that night to pack my clothes
                    and gun.   30

I stopped to think how Rose would feel and what Ike would
                    have to say,
But still I packed my shit that night to make my getaway.

Dolly said to me, "Daddy, are we ready to roll?"
I heard a shot and slid to my knees. The ground was
                    very cold.

I heard a scream, a shuffle of feet, and I heard
                    somebody say
That the cops were on the scene, but the gunman had
                    got away.

I woke up in a hospital ward in a prison called
                    "The Well,"[1]
And all the hacks were standing around to hear what
                    I had to tell.

But how could I say it was my best friend and that I'd tried
                    to steal his play,
That he had shot me down that night trying to make
                    my getaway?   40

So if you ever hope to cross a pal, and I hope you never will,
Remember what happened to the Thoroughbred Kid that came
                    from Sugar Hill.[2]

[1]Bridewell jail, in Chicago.

[2]Zora Neale Hurston (1942:96) identifies Sugar Hill as follows: "northwest corner of Harlem, near Washington Heights, site of newest apartment houses, mostly occupied by professional people. (The expression has been distorted in the South to mean a Negro red light district.)"

BROADWAY SAM

Toast heroes are victims not only of outside forces like a narco's trap but also of personal weaknesses. The narrator of "The Fall" is destroyed by his own addiction and his whore's unwillingness to relinquish him; Good-Doing Wheeler falls because of his main man's weakness for cheap wine; Dumbo is shattered by his girl's betrayal; and the Thoroughbred Kid by his own. But no protagonist in the toasts falls so far as Broadway Sam.

Although homosexuality shows its pale face from time to time in the repertoire, it is usually apparent only in the nicknames of peripheral characters. With Sam it is the nadir of his personal defeat, and when, after such a falling-off as that, "they found him dead, garbage under his head," we are not surprised. No apologies are made for Sam: though the narrator clearly respects him and "almost cried the day he died," he has nothing but contempt for the addiction which brought him down.

This is another of Superjunkie's drug-related toasts, recited in 1958 in Clinton. He claimed it was a true story and that he had known its author, from whom he had learned it "a few years back."

Broadway Sam

Broadway Sam, the big mackman—
    Yes, I know the name.
I almost cried the day he died.
    It was a dirty shame.

He liked to play on old Broadway;
    That's how he got his name.
He lived off the hicks from out in the sticks.
    He was a master of the long-shoe game.

He was always pressed; nothing but the best
    Vines and kicks he had;   10
A thirty-dollar lid and gloves of kid—
    Man, his threads were bad—

White-on-whites and black skin-tights
    And a belt of pure crocodile.
When he stepped out, all the whores would shout,
    But Sam—why, he'd just smile.

He was riding high, the limit was the sky.
    He had all kinds of dough.
But he became a junky, a low-down flunky,
    When he pulled a dope fiend whore.   20

Her name was Mable, and she was able
    To turn eight kinds of tricks.
You'd flip your lid over that kid
    If you were a hick from the sticks.

She was the best in the East and the West,
    Once, a long time ago,
But an arm full of junk will take all the spunk
    Out of the very best whore.

She said, "Hey, Baby, I don't mean maybe,
    Give this stuff a try."   30
So he blew his fame, he lost the game,
    He went and got himself high.

He was king of them all till he took that fall,
    Till he made that fatal slip.
He thought it was boss when he shot that horse;
    He thought he was being hip.

Two months it took till he got hooked
    On the pleasure of the kings.
When he got caught with his money short,
    He had to hock his things.   40

He pawned his clothes, he lost his whores,
    He really did come down.
The king of them all had started his fall.
    The king had lost his crown.

His clothes were tattered, but that didn't matter—
    Not to Sam, at least,
As long as Mable his whore was able
    To satisfy his beast.

When she went to jail, Sam had no bail
    To cut old Mable loose.   50
It was there and then the moment when
    Sam just cooked his goose.

Without his whore to bring him dough
    Sam started to get sick.
He got so sick he sucked a dick.
    Big Sam had turned a trick.

Yes, Broadway Sam, the big mackman,
    Had really fallen down.
He was Sam the fag, in or out of drag,
    The funkiest junky in town.   60

They found him dead, garbage under his head,
    Out behind a store.
That faggot Sam, the used-to-be man,
    Had his asshole tore.

Just what went down in that part of town
    On that terrible night
No one knows, but some suppose
    That he just lost a fight.

But I don't buy that, I know where it's at—
    He died of an overdose.   70
And every night when the moon is bright,
    You can see his ghost.

On old Broadway where he used to play
    He moans his way around,
Looking for Mable, the whore that was able—
    The bitch that brought him down.

Yes, I knew him, and the broad that slew him—
    Mable was her name.
He played the Game, and he searched for fame,
    But a faggot he died in shame.   80

THE JUNKIE

"The Junkie" shows us the lower depths of the Life. Its self-pitying narrator is not really a player; he is a derelict whose ambition soars no higher than to snatch a purse, and who fumbles even that. He is only on the fringes of the Life, so sunk in his addiction that he exhibits neither regret nor hope.

Toasts seldom deal in a realistic way with success, and when they do, it is usually with such successes as that of the junkie here: the theft of enough for a fix.

Superjunkie recited this one at the same session as the last. Nothing else in his repertoire showed the life of the addict in so mercilessly bleak a light, and he was at pains to assure his audience that the toast was merely a warning to the unwary and not a personal anecdote.

The Junkie

I'll always remember one cold December
    When my feet was on the ground.
I was beaten and hadn't eaten,
    And there wasn't a friend around.

Now after my toes was almost froze,
    I stumbled into an inn.
Barkeep started to shout, "No hanging about—
    Get on out to the snow again."

I felt abused and much misused.
    How could a man be so mean?   10
Couldn't he see I was beat to one knee,
    That I was just a poor dope fiend?

Again the snow was between each toe,
    And I was going God knows where.
I'd have felt more jolly could I have taken the trolley,
    But I just didn't have the fare.

Then I saw a young girl who was out of this world,
    With her purse swinging real nice.
I got ready to swing and snatch that thing,
    But fate had me slip on the ice.   20

Gee, I was mad. My luck was so bad!
    You should have heard me curse.
If that broad hadn't run, I'd have got up and done
    What I had flunked at first.

A poolroom was near, so I started in there
    To get in out of the cold and wet.
I stood real shy, hoping some guy
    Would ask me to hold a bet.

It was just as I planned. With ten in my hand,
    And the two lanes chalking their stick,   30
I coughed real loud and stepped up proud
    And went out the door to spit.

Now you know I was gone when them lanes caught on
    That I had done them harm.
I was laying up in my pad, no longer sad,
    With a spike sunk deep in my arm.

KONKY MOHAIR

"Konky Mohair" was evidently inspired in part by "Honky-Tonk Bud," whose hero appears in lines 99–100; indeed, the first stanza is patterned so closely on that of its model as to be almost a parody. But there are crucial differences between "Konky" and the two Honky-Tonk Bud poems after the first four lines: the controlled diction and urbane, ironic point of view of the present poem clearly distinguish it from the Bud poems and in fact from all others in the collection.

"Konky Mohair" employs several devices not usually found in toasts: a recurring line (1, 25, 41, 69, 113, 133); a shadow of incremental repetition (11. 89–91); an extended flashback concluded with a narrative flourish (1. 105); and an ending unparalleled in the literature of the Life. The poem shares many features with other toasts. Its hero serves an apprentice-ship like Dumbo and Honky-Tonk Bud; he comments on the deterioration of his profession like the narrator of "The Fall"; he goes to prison and is unable to cope with changed circumstances on his release like Good-Doing Wheeler. But his bodily Assumption and canonization are unique.

This was recited by Washington in 1962. He had brought it to Attica, along with the rest of his repertoire, from one of the juvenile institutions in New York where, he said, toasts flourish.

Konky Mohair

Konky Mohair, the poor man's square,
    Was digging a game of chance.
While the action was lagging and the dice was dragging,
    He kept his feet down in his pants.

For he knew well enough that times was rough,
 And lately he'd been in a rut.
As facts are mattered, his luck was shattered,
 For he was what you'd call "on the nut."

Now the few coins he numbered as being his own
 Were precious and not for the gamble: 10
A dime and a quarter to nourish his bones
 And a token in case he would ramble.

His back was bent from a coat that was lent
 By a dealer in paper and rags.
His sky was new—in 1942—
 And his shoes were two-toned drags.

He had a belt that was made from the Lone Ranger's mount,
 Worth neither pig nor a poke,
And his pants was down and out for the count—
 Each leg was going for broke.   20

Why, if the rollers had showed to make things tough
 And saw what all could see,
They'd have saved Konky Mohair by locking him up
 And letting all the dice players go free.

Now Konky Mohair, the poor man's square,
 Had once known better days.
He was young and fly, frisky and spry,
 And hip to those fast-money ways.

A topnotch pimp, name of Kansas City Gimp,
 Taught him all the tricks of the trade.   30
In no time at all Konky got on the ball
 And had ten whores—nine pinks and a shade.

There was Slump-Rump Flora, a blonde from Dannemora,
 Dribble-Hips and Soft-Belly Sue;
There was Pump-'n'-Grind Fanny and Sweet-Lip Annie,
 Who dug just what she had to do;

There was a redhead named Linda and an Arab
               named Lucinda,
  Both famous for their many works of art,
And a coal-black goddess name of Tutti-Frutti Doris
    Who could make Campbell's beans forget how to fart. 40

Konky Mohair, the poor man's square,
    Was king of all the whores.
He had all the money in the world
    And a mansion full of clothes.

But the whores grew cold, as whores will do,
    And trouble came Konky's way.
All along the avenue
    The tricks refused to pay.

"I pays my money, and I makes my choice,"
    Was the word upon the air.   50
What did they care for Konky Mohair
    Or the knowledge that he was fair?

No longer able to play the Game,
    Konky called a tremendous meeting.
He praised all his people for being cool,
    But his funds was taking a beating.

"I've always been fair with my people;
    I always abide by the rules.
Now the young whores is trying to outslick me,
    And the tricks are no longer fools.   60

"The police keep their feet in my pocket;
    Bartenders grin when I show.
Life ran a feature, then charged me;
    My name was too much in the know."

So saying he closed the meeting,
 And all the whores dispersed.
They scattered across the nation,
 And prostitution was at its worst.

Now Konky Mohair, the poor man's square,
 Bought a large piece of cocaine.   70
He knew his fortune was surely made
 If he didn't do business with lanes.

Things went fast for quite a spell,
 Success with a leap and a bound.
From Timbuctoo to London Dell
 They toasted the best girl in town.

Hustlers came from far-off lands
 To purchase his cocaine.
Gabardine Willie came by ship,
 Stick Pin came by train.   80

Boosting Sam from out of St. Louis,
 Dip-Dip from Chicago way,
And a big numbers banker, name of Dirty-Money Tanker,
 Showed with a whole year's play.

His riches were steady increasing,
 His name was more famous than Ike's.
He would oftentimes give those boss sessions—
 You know, the kind we all like.

No doubt he was the most popular.
 No doubt he was the most kind.   90
No doubt he was informed on.
 You can bet he had to do that dime.

Now Konky Mohair, the poor man's square,
 Was home after years away.
The scene was weird, the people strange,
 And things had all gone astray.

The whores were all using poison;
    The informer was king of the street.
Even Honky-Tonk Bud, the Hipcat Stud,
    Was eating shit for meat.   100

Konky looked all around him
    And dug how it all shaped up.
He vowed that before he'd turn around
    He'd play behind shades, cane, and cup.

Now Konky was where we just left him.
    Remember? Digging that game of chance.
But his thoughts weren't on the action,
    So his feet remained in his pants.

The players were all johnny-come-latelies,
    Not known for deeds of good.   110
They'd boast of royal pedigrees,
    But not a heart beat like a thoroughbred's should.

Now Konky Mohair, the poor man's square,
    Shuffled away from the game.
As said before and repeated many score,
    His appearance was a drag and a shame.

But good fortune smiled upon him
    Before he paced many feet,
And a tremendous light engulfed him
    As he wandered down the street.   120

A chariot made of solid gold
    Pulled by ten Cadillacs full of money
And ten gorgeous girls from around the world
    With milk and cream and honey;

A young Greek boy playing "Things To Come"
    (That's a side by Diz and Bird),[1]
And Ava Gardner on her hands and knees,
    Shitting a cocaine turd;

A fine young jasper with sixty-inch thighs
    And tits squirting sweet muscatel;   130
A girl soft as jelly, dancing on her belly,
    While thirty reefers played "Godchild" on one bell.

Konky Mohair, the poor man's square,
    Was whisked away into the night.
His legend grew as legends do,
    But this much I can add if I might:

When hustlers are dealing in zeroes
    And thoroughbreds treated unfair,
They all take a drag on their reefers
    And say prayers to St. Konky Mohair.   140

[1]John Birks "Dizzy" Gillespie (1917–), trumpeter, and Charles "Bird" Parker (1920–1955), alto saxophonist—jazz virtuosi.

THE BALL OF THE FREAKS

Toasts are frequently vulgar, but they are never pornographic; prurience is wholly alien to the genre. Generally, sex is referred to, as in "The Fall," only as a commodity, and the tone in which it is described is one of professional appreciation; the pimp views a whore's skills as an impresario views a dancer's. The only toast devoted entirely to orgiastic behavior is "The Ball of the Freaks," but this robust doggerel has none of the sly spirit of pornography. It is an extended exercise in scatology.

"The Ball of the Freaks" may, as Abrahams suggests (1970: 167), owe something to "The Darktown Strutters' Ball," but it seems to have a closer affinity to that classic of Scottish bawdry "The Ball o' Kirriemuir," from whose title it may have adopted the peculiar syntax of its own. According to James Barke (1959: 32–33), "The Ball o' Kirriemuir" supposedly celebrates a real event of the 1880's in the Kirriemuir district of Scotland and "developed from a twenty-verse work to its present-day form, in which there are hundreds of verses and innumerable variants. Two world wars spread it among the personnel of the services, and they added and subtracted and amended until today the thing is without beginning or end."

"The Ball of the Freaks" is similarly infinite and infinitely adaptable; it accommodates snatches of popular songs, altered to its theme, and it incorporates every prosodic form from the freest of verse to the ballad quatrain with internal rhyme. It may be recited by the hour, with everyone in the crowd contributing bits, remembered or improvised, as he thinks of them. And any clear narrative line it may once have contained has been hopelessly submerged, like that of its Scottish forerunner. "The Ball of the Freaks" survives, unique in its type, as a grab bag.

Essentially a boy's toast, "The Ball of the Freaks" is known very widely but seldom recited after adolescence. Everyone has his own version, and no one pretends his is complete. The one given here was taken down from Bob in Sing Sing in 1954, but there was little difference between his version and those of others sitting with him at the performance; others chimed in lines as he progressed, and he gladly incorporated them into his own recitation. Bob was a black New Yorker around twenty and couldn't remember where he had first heard "The Ball of the Freaks"; in fact, he couldn't remember a time when he hadn't known it.

The Ball of the Freaks

A cold misty rain fell on Spokane,
    The red-light city of the Coast,
Where the whores get high on cocaine
    And stand on the corners and boast

About pimps and chumps from back-alley dumps
    That made their rise to fame
And the parties they threw, which were quite a few,
    In the life they call the Game.

Old Fast-Fucking Fannie told Cripple-Tongue Annie,
    "Mama, let's give a session tonight."   10
She spoke of a gig that would last for weeks,
    And that's how it came about, the Ball of the Freaks.

They invited red-headed Flo, a notorious whore,
    And a bitch named Light-Fingered Peggy Malone,
Whose face was scarred, and her cunt was marred,
    And her fingers calloused to the bone.

They imported Shit-Eating Willy from up in
              North Philly
    And another whore named Grace.
Grace was a sadist, one of the maddest,
    Who'd freak off in the good Lord's face.   20

There was a jasper named Nora and a bitch
                    named Dora,
    But the nastiest slut of them all
Was a tramp named Roberta, and disease couldn't
                    hurt her,
    So they crowned her Queen of the Ball.

There was a crowd in the kitchen, a mob in the hall,
    A short-arm inspection by the shithouse wall.
Long-Shoe Sam and Cocaine Smitty
    Brought a bunch of faggots from New York City.

They had fancy trimmings and ball-twisting women
    And homos that died for dicks,   30
Cocksuckers by the dozens, motherfuckers and
                    their cousins,
Porkchop- and peppermint-flavored pricks.

There was old Fart-Smelling Rosie, acting kind of nosy,
    Sniffing real hard for some gas;
Towel-Slinging Kelly, whose ass looked like jelly
    From being popped so much in the past.

When someone farted, Rosie shouted,
    "Leave it alone, it's mine!"
And off she went to pick up the scent
    With her nose up some freak's behind.   40

There was Graveyard Monk, who sucked dead cunt
    And had once been buried in a grave.
He had a whore he'd dug up a month ago
    Whose flesh was nine years decayed.

"Hot damn!" cried the faggots as they dug the maggots
    Crawling out that bitch's hips,
But old Monk only pressed the corpse to his chest
    And sucked some worms from her tits.

Now while the nymphos were looking for something to do,
In walked three dudes all dressed in blue: 50
Wolf Man, Dracula, and Hunchback too.

Hunch went to the corner, 'cause he knew his place;
He was a freak for having *something* shit in his face.

Old Wolf Man hung like a whore with a kitchen
                              clothes line
While Dracula sucked blood from a homo's spine.
Then in the doorway stepped Frankenstein.

He said, "I'm raggedy and I'm down,
Wasn't invited but I came around.

"Lord, I'm so happy I could jump, shit, and shout.
Now let's see one you bad-breath motherfuckers put
                              me out."   60

He grabbed a one-eye bitch with the seven-year itch
       And threw her toes to the ceiling.
The action was like a flash, her cunt opened like
                              a gash,
       And her brown-eye lost all its feeling.

"Franky, Franky," she cried as she almost died,
       "Franky, please have a heart.
My ass is torn, my cunt is worn—
       You're ripping my insides apart."

But old Franky only laughed, 'cause he was coming
                              at last,
       And his swipe swole twice its size.   70
His rich hot come made the bitch's body numb,
       And the whore went blind in both eyes.

She moaned and she farted and shit on the floor,
And the wind from her asshole blew the doorknob off
                    the door.

That's when that bitch Nell let out a big yell
        And shitted all over the bed.
In the dining room Willy copped a spoon
        And a half a loaf of bread.

While in the kitchen, Willy spied the Hunch
Sucking the innards out of a dead whore's cunt.   80

The air was rancid and full of come.
Only a man could stand it in an iron lung.

The shit was so thick it made Dracula sick.
Three snorts of that air made vet junkies kick.

It made some drunk and unable to walk.
One whore was eating pig pussy and calling it pork.

They had fried shit choplets and hot funk custard,
Drank spit out of cocktail glasses and used afterbirth
                    for mustard.

They ate hot farts cut into four parts,
Maggot pies sprinkled with guebe dust,   90
Dipped in piss and soaked with pus.

Boiled dicks, fried dicks, dicks without bones,
Slimy potato salad which no one left alone.

Along about ten, three weeks from then,
        The ball came to an end.
But they sucked and farted, fucked and parted,
        Like true freaks to the bitter end.

WISE EGG

"Wise Egg" is a fragmentary narrative whose penultimate line places it with such toasts as "Kitty Barrett," "The Fall," and "Sugar Hill"—pieces conceived as spoken in prison. It might serve as a flashback in some long first-person story.

Its speaker is the traditional non-specialized player who has robbed, blown safes, pimped, and swindled rich whites. He glories in his versatility, which includes such unlikely legitimate talents as roping bulls and waiting on tables. Bruce Jackson (1965A:324) rightly calls it a "hobo narrative at heart."

Like "Sugar Hill," this toast has the rare feature of regret, but of a much more conventional sort than the Thoroughbred Kid's. The speaker merely attaches the classic warning formula of the old murderer-ballad to his first stanza. Jackson's version (1965A:323–324) ends with a repetition of the moral-warning, but the wise egg speaking in our version is clearly unrepentant; his last words express his resolve, like that implicit in the last two lines of "The Fall," to return to his former ways as soon as he gets out of prison.

Pop, who recited this in Auburn in 1967, is the oldest inmate represented in this collection. A black in his fifties, Pop had served time off and on since the late 1920's and claimed to have seen the deterioration of the moral standards of the Life since then. He said he had learned "Wise Egg" during the Depression.

Wise Egg

I once was a wise egg; I would lie, steal, or beg,
  And was never afraid of a fall.
But all you slick guys who consider yourselves wise
  Should take heed and avoid your downfall.

The last job I pulled I got caught blowing the lock on
                          a jewelry store.
They beat me to my knees and put me on the stand to
                          declare war.

Well, I didn't have the gift of gab; so I was like a
                          ditty bop lost in a fog.
I might have gotten away, but the bluecoat mob was
                          on the job.

I didn't give a fuck about being in a sling,
'Cause I knew my name, and I knew how it ringed.   10

I was called the meanest man in town.
I had taken a ride to Liverpool just to lay
                          the larceny down.

Why, I had roped bulls on the Wyoming track
And taught Honky-Tonk Bud the mack.

I'd carried a tray in a New York café,
    Hopped bells in the hotels of Chi,
Tapped spikes beside the spics,
    And caught redball freights on the fly.

I've walked and talked with the Duke of York
    And danced with the Duchess of Kent.   20
But, Jim, the weather was cool in Liverpool,
    Where I took off the great Jay Gould.

Why, I took a trip to France just to steal me five
                          hundred pounds,
And with a taxi and two French girls I took in every
                          cabaret in town.

It was just about one when I ended my fun;
    Being broke was very seldom.
That's when I like to have lost my life over that
                          square john's wife
    For playing so hard in Belgium.

I guess I should go to church like them other fellows
  And try to save my sinful soul,   30
But I fooled the Germans with Protestant sermons
  And made Hitler pay off in gold.

They searched every steamer when I beat Mussolini,
  But they couldn't find a trace of me.
For me and One Lung and Chinese Lee
  Were down underground smoking tea.

Yes, I've been as low as a man can go,
  And now, I declare it's a sin.
Let me finish this bit, and give me some shit,
  Call me Lucky, and I'm gone again.   40

DEATH ROW

Prison serves a socializing function for many of the younger and less adept in the Life, allowing them to share their ideas and experiences and, of course, learn each other's toasts. It is not surprising, then, that some toasts deal specifically with prison and have only a slender relation to the Life. The two toasts which follow belong to this group.

"Death Row" is on balance a product and expression of the Life, rather than of prison culture, although most of its jargon is common to all prison inmates in New York. Greasy Jim's choice of food—collard greens, lobster Newburgh, and pheasant under glass—as well as the flashback to his former life (ll. 29–40)—show him to be a player. But more significant yet is the tone of defiant bravado in the first sixty lines. It is only at line 61 that we begin to see the poem for what it is: an ironic comment on that icy composure and swagger. Like most of the other humorous toasts, "Death Row" is in some respects a lampoon of the Life.

The outrageous trick in the last ten lines can be made defensible by good recitation; a skilled teller will deliver the first sixty lines with contemptuous self-assurance, the next twenty-two in an increasingly desperate and feminine whine, and the ending in an altered voice dripping with incredulity and disgust. It is said to get a laugh even on death row.

This version, the longest one encountered, was delivered by Otto in Sing Sing in 1953. That institution still had the electric chair in 1953; and though Otto had never occupied a cell on death row, he claimed to have worked there cleaning the gallery and to have heard the toast recited there in the late 1940's. Otto was one of the few whites heard reciting toasts. A long-time inmate of Sing Sing, he had learned many in that prison and said that he had heard this one from an old black awaiting execution.

Death Row

Well, they fried Tough Tony last night,
The man who didn't know the meaning of fright.

He was the dude who wasn't afraid to die,
But we all heard that big faggot cry.

He broke down and cried like a scared little bitch
And begged them not to throw the switch.

Today's June first, today I go—
Today's my turn to be the star of the show.

Then comes Jojo and then Big Red,
But the main event's over after I'm dead.   10

There'll be lights and cameras and plenty of action
And Greasy Jim the main attraction.

There won't be no crying or copping no pleas,
Hanging on the bars or begging on my knees.

When it comes my time to walk that wing,
I'll hold my head high like an ancient king.

They fed us last night and said it's our last;
Jojo threw his up, and Red took his fast.

I downed the collard greens, the T-bone steak,
Heavy on the gravy, and a big piece of cake.   20

Lobster à la Newburgh, pheasant under glass,
And I didn't let a goddamn crumb get past.

When I cracked for seconds, the hack stood
                    there looking.
I said, "Serve it raw, punk. The chair'll do
                    the cooking."

I went back to my cell and laid down on my bed
And rubbed my hand over my bald head.

I lay back on my bunk, trying to smoke,
And listened to a hack tell a dirty joke.

My mind drifted back to my woman on the street.
I heard she was using stuff and looking kind of beat.   30

I heard she was going with my main man Moose,
Who turned her into a stomp-down whore and then cut
                    her loose.

All in all, I wouldn't mind it so,
But the fact is, I'd robbed and killed for this whore.

I can still remember the day I shot that storekeeper
                    dead.
I said, "Freeze, motherfucker, and just give me that
                    bread."

He started to scream and simply wouldn't cease,
So I popped four caps through his chest with my piece.

And in making my exit, I iced a cop
'Cause the motherfucker shot at me when
                    I wouldn't stop.   40

But those are memories from long before my trial,
And now it's time to walk that last mile.

Soon I heard a noise coming down the hall.
I looked up and seen a shadow on the wall.

Who's that with the funny white collar band?
What's that, a short-heist book in his hand?

Oh, that's you, old Father Brown.
I don't know why in hell you keep coming 'round.

I don't want to hear about resurrection of Easter.
You can shove that Bible up your kiester.   50

Every time you speak of dying, it only brings anger
                              to my heart.
Can't you see the gates are opening and the show's
                              about to start?

The Warden says to the Reverend, "Father, this man's
                              a fool."
I said, "Dig yourself, creep, don't lose your cool."

Soon it comes time to take me away.
There doesn't seem anything else to say.

Now I give my regards to all Death Row.
"Take it easy, Rabbit. I'll see you later, Joe.

"So long, Jojo. Good-bye, Freddie.
No tears for me, Red. I told you I was ready."   60

When we reach the green door, I happen to look in.
I didn't mind the silence, but the lights were
                              so goddamn dim.

I saw my legal aid standing there,
Looking like he thought the whole damn thing was fair.

I thought, maybe a reprieve, maybe good news.
Maybe the electric chair blew a fuse.

No reprieve? No news? The chair's in good order?
Where's the hack? Call the Warden. I need a glass
                              of water.

"Guards, guards, I'm dying of thirst.
Let Big Red or Jojo go first."   70

I tried to fight, I tried to resist,
But the suckers were too big, they twisted down my wrist.

"Father Brown, Father Brown, please say you will—
Tell the Warden I was a good kid who didn't mean
                    to kill."

Father Brown walked over and pulled up a chair,
Whipped out his book and read off a prayer.

He said, "Forgive this man, he knows not what he did."
I said, "Can that shit, Father; don't let them burn
                    the kid."

I screamed, I stomped; I raved and cursed.
"What's wrong with Jojo? Why not let Red go first?   80

"Somebody, please, unstrap my wrist.
I want to, I got to, I need to take a piss."
                    •   •   •
"Hey, Rabbit, did you hear that scream?"
"Yeah, but it can't be Jim. He's too damn mean."

"But I swear I recognized his voice."
"Yeah, but it sounded like my sister Joyce."

Just then a hack came and ran down this tale
Of how Jim turned stone pussy and screamed and wailed.

How he called for his ma, begged for his pa,
Gave up all the connections and then called Allah.[1]   90

But what makes it so bad, the dirty son of a bitch
Died of fright before they could pull the switch.

---

[1]Because *Allah* is stressed on the last syllable by Black Muslims (a lá), this line rhymes
and scans perfectly.

BILL AND LIL

This little joke of a toast is especially popular among young people and indeed reflects an adolescent view of the Life. Bill expects continued loyalty and support from his woman and is furious at her defection.

It is one of the fondest myths of the Life that a pimp can, like Honky-Tonk Bud, depend on his women to remain humble chattels while he is in prison. In fact, the response of Lil and the author of "The Letter" is rather the rule, and it is only because toasts are a male genre that men always get revenge and have the last word in them.

Bob delivered this toast in Sing Sing in 1954. He said he picked it up in Elmira, one of the New York State correctional facilities for juvenile offenders.

Bill And Lil

Dear Lil:
  I'm sitting here in this man-made hell,
Thinking of nature's beauty from my prison cell.

Wondering how life is treating you
And why your letters are so short and few.

Girl, you swore you'd write me each day
And fix it so I'd give the commissary a steady play.

But ten long years of bitter regret
Won't stop me busting your ass when I get back on
                    the set.
            •   •   •
Dear Bill:
  Why, you dizzy motherfucker,
How long you going to be a sucker?   10

I was your woman, and not your wife;[1]
So you fuck with me and I'll have you doing life.

Me and your man just pulled off a sting,
And I'm not sending you a goddamn thing.

•   •   •

Dear Lil:
    I read your latest mail,
And I must admit it left me pale.

But I'll do this bit on sheer determination,
And when I get out I'll plan your extermination.

•   •   •

Dear Punk:
    I read your letter, and you're becoming a bore.
Please don't write me any more.   20

•   •   •

Dear Lil:
    The Warden went swimming today
And brought me with him to watch him play.

But after a while he almost drowned,
And I saved his life the third trip down.

For being so very brave and bold,
He just decided to give me a parole.

•   •   •

Dear Bill:
    This is Lil's brother Jack.
Lil just died of a heart attack,

And being that you loved each other so,
I thought you should be the first to know.   30

•   •   •

---

[1]Possibly a reference to the law prohibiting the admission of the testimony of a spouse in court; since she was not his legal wife, Lil could testify against him.

Dear Jack:

I got your letter concerning Lil's death.
Tell me, were you there when she took her last breath?

If so, young man, then in your time
You have witnessed the perfect crime.

BAD DAN

The sources of toasts are often impossible to determine because the material is adapted beyond recognition. Slaves learned the Scottish and Irish border ballads sung by their owners and reworked them into their own lives, and popular songs and local ballads like "John Henry" found their way into the toast repertoire. Whatever is attractive to the community in this diverse material is employed in the formation of new poems. The Wild West and the Old South have been rich sources for this grafting process.

A Western badman piece included among toasts because of its diction and its reflection of the value system of the Life, "Bad Dan" is something of an alien. The protagonist admits to rural residency and hard work, either of which would disqualify him for the Life: "My home is the backwoods, where I work like a slave" (1. 21). But his virility and braggadocio have an appeal for players which has won this piece a place in the repertoire. The tall tale elements (11. 14–20) are clearly importations, but something in their spirit is seen in "The Return of Honky-Tonk Bud." Toasts like "Bad Dan" and the two which follow it here, "Badman Dan and Two-Gun Green" and "Bill Skinner," are immigrants into the Life, stories which come from other cultures but which have been naturalized. Their language and attitudes show the naturalization, but the origin in Western tall tales remains apparent.

Duke delivered all three of these pieces in Auburn in 1964. He said that he had learned them from an old-time player he had met in the Merchant Marine during the 50's.

Bad Dan

Back in the days of '34,
They were snatching cunts across the floor,
Spreading joy forever more.

Now in the corner sat big Bad Dan,
The baddest, cruellest motherfucker in the land,

Playing blackjack, short on blues,
A game all bad motherfuckers were booked to lose.

"No wonder my luck is so bad tonight.
There's a stranger standing between me and the light.

"Say, there, stranger, know who I am?"   10
Stranger replied, "Don't give a damn."

Then Dan replied, "Before you die,
I'll tell you the pedigree of my life.

"I got sixteen inches across my chest,
I don't bar a thing, sickness or death.

"I ride a lion bareback,
Beating his ass with a blackjack,
Daring him to look back.

"I ride the thunder without a veil,
Handcuff lightning, throw thunder in jail.

"My home is the backwoods, where I work like a slave.   20
Fucking and fighting is all I crave.

"Smashing windows, kicking down doors,
Mistreating good women and calling them whores.

"When I marry, I'm going to marry a cow,
So I can fuck, buck, suck, milk, and plow."

Then when the view was blocked by a whore
Billy Clapshit pulled out his Colt .44.

There was shriek, a bang, a sudden cough,
And all the lights suddenly went off.

Bad Dan emerged from the gloom,
Slamming the door to the torn-up room.   30

"If they ask you what the riot's about,
Tell them Billy Clapshit just checked out."

BADMAN DAN AND TWO-GUN GREEN

Another outsider uncomfortably residing in the Life, "Badman Dan" contains some of the same Western elements as "Bad Dan." The tall boasts (11. 63–70), for example, are as out of keeping with the Life as those of the preceding toast but nevertheless popular. This toast contains more of the true Life spirit, however: the variety of sexual reference (oral sex 11. 7–8, 25, 29, 32; anal sex 1. 20; homosexuality 11. 47, 58), the catalogue of humorously named characters unrelated to the story (11. 7–20), and the general atmosphere of the bar before the fight are all typical features of the city toast. Two-Gun Green is mentioned in "The Return of Honky-Tonk Bud" (11. 269–272).

Recited by Duke in Auburn, 1964.

Badman Dan And Two-Gun Green

It was a cold windy night in New Orleans
When Badman Dan met Two-Gun Green.

I was tending bar, I'll never forget.
It was the Bucket of Blood where the two first met.

There were hustlers and suckers from near and far,
And money-making johnnies stood four at the bar.

There was Juicy-Lip Lil in the corner with a trick,
Slobbing like a mule with a mouth full of dick.

In another corner, calm and serene,
Sat that bad motherfucker, Two-Gun Green.   10

Harry the faggot was bleeding from the ass
'Cause he'd backed up to a dick just a little too fast.

At the end of the bar stood Lily McDrum;
A wiggle from her ass made dead men come.

Money John was snatching a whore's arm out of the socket
'Cause he caught her hand in his motherfucking
                    money-making pocket.

When out of the crowd and onto the floor
Came a bitch known to all as a stomp-down whore.

She answered to the name of Mary Brown,
And that bitch made all the money in the whole
                    fucking town.   20

Now as she danced to the beat of the band,
The clock struck one, and the shit began.

In walked Bad Dan. You could tell he was high.
He had his dick in his hand and a gleam in his eye.

He said, "Come here, bitch, and give me some head.
'Cause if you don't, I'll slap you dead."

She said, "All right, Dan, you don't have to shout.
Just let your money beat your big dick out.

"You can get some cunt, asshole, or head,
As long as you got the motherfucking bread."   30

He said, "Listen, bitch, around here my word's law.
Now give me some head, or I'll crack your motherfucking
                    jaw."

She said, "If you do, you'll be dead. If you think
                    you're so mean,
Come talk to my man, Mr. Two-Gun Green."

Now Dan's voice was like a thundering bass,
And his arm slipped from around the bitch's ass.

He said, "What motherfucker here professes to be
As rough and tough and as bad as me?

"Just let this motherfucker stand,"
Rumbled the voice of Badman Dan.   40

The cats around the bar were filled with fright,
'Cause they knew Dan was bad and looking for a fight.

He grabbed the nearest punk in sight
And cracked his jaw with an overhand right.

He knocked another one with a mighty crash
And stomped to the bar a'kicking ass.

He shit on the faggots and spit on the whores,
Broke all the chairs and knocked down the doors.

He drank all the whisky, broke all the glass,
Vaulted the bar and kicked *me*, the barkeep,
                              in the ass.   50

Cats was jumping out the windows and running out
                              the doors.
Dan wasn't doing nothing but dropping pimps' whores.

He threw tables and chairs all over the place,
Walked up to Green and looked him dead in the face.

He said, "You must be this new punk in town
That's got this bitch named Mary Brown.

"Well, I'll fuck you up with a cause.
I'll fuck your whore and make *you* drop your drawers.

"So sit down, faggot, and listen to me
While I run down my pedigree.   60

"I'll have you know I'm Badman Dan,
The baddest motherfucker in all this land.

"I was born in a barrel of butcher knives,
Raised between two .45's.

"I eat raw polar bear meat, and, needless to say,
I swim to the North Pole three times a day.

"My mother was a harlot, my father a thriller,
I got two sisters and a brother, and, Jim, they're all
real killers.

"I walk a barbed-wire fence, a tiger in each hand.
I'm that bad motherfucker, Badman Dan.   70

"So you see, motherfucker, you're out of luck."
Now up jumped Green saying, "I don't give a fuck.

"Now sit down, mister, and listen to me,
While I run down *my* pedigree.

"I'll have you know I'm Two-Gun Green,
The baddest motherfucker the world has ever seen.

"I was weaned off the tit of a wild boar,
And I cut my teeth on a Colt .44.

"I can be mean without even trying.
I'm a bad motherfucker, and I don't mind dying.   80

"I walked a thousand miles through the sunny South
Just to punch one jive motherfucker in the mouth.

"Human blood is my food, poison is my wine.
When I wake up evil, I dare the sun to shine.

"I've handcuffed lightning, shackled thunder,
Walked through a graveyard and put the dead to wonder.

"I've fucked a she-lion, dared the he-lion to roar,
And fucked *him* in the ass when I felt like more.

"Took some cunt from a gorilla, a hell of a trick—
I had to sandpaper her ass down to fit my dick.   90

"If I catch you fucking with my whore,
I'll make room in my private graveyard for just
                    one more."

Dan made his pass at those last words,
And Green's two .44's was the last sound he heard.

Believe me, Jim, this is no lie:
Dan went down with two bullets in his
                    motherfucking eye.

BILL SKINNER

The story of "Bill Skinner," like those of the two preceding toasts, is not characteristic of the Life; for one thing, neither women nor drugs is mentioned here. But several features mark "Bill Skinner" as unquestionably black, even if it came to the community from the white pioneer culture. The game to which it refers is cooncan, for example, and one of the two characters hails, like the Thoroughbred Kid, from Sugar Hill in Harlem.

Recited by Duke in Auburn, 1964.

Bill Skinner

Bill Skinner was a gambler's name.
With cards and dice he won his fame.

He was a dice shooter and a blackjack man,
Loved to shoot craps and spread cooncan.

He played with the best from coast to coast,
The way gambler Bill's name called for a toast.

There was only one man who could whip old Bill,
Cooncan Malone from Sugar Hill.

The first and last bet the Bill ever lost
He was spreading against Malone, the cooncan boss.   10

They were getting down heavy and letting the
                    pots ride,
And us fellows were making a few simple bets on
                    the side.

In shirtsleeves they sat, watching each spread,
Both boys cool but their eyes blood red.

About daybreak that morning Bill made his last bet,
Nervous, groggy, and wringing wet.

Well, it was time to be nervous, for he'd lost all
                    he had,
About 200 grand and a fine string of pads.

Malone got up and started to go,
But Bill knocked him down as he reached the floor.   20

Malone stood there with a gat in his hand,
And Bill snatched a cleaver, and they stood man to man.

A shot rang out as Malone stepped back,
And with cleaver in hand Bill started to hack.

When it was over, both boys were dead,
Bill minus his face and Malone his head.

Now Bill took a chance like some gamblers do,
But he was a sore loser, just like a few.

Now he'll play no more cards nor shoot any dice,
For the first and last bet he lost put him on ice.   30

STAGGER LEE

The proto-toast "Stacker Lee" (also recorded as "Stackalee," "Stackolee," "Stagolee," "Stagalee," etc.) has been widely printed and discussed since a version of it appeared in the *Journal of American Folklore* in 1911 (*JAF* XXIV: 228). The Lomaxes (1934: 93–99) give two versions of the song and some suggestions about its origins. Abrahams (1970C:129–42) has amply summarized the literature of the ballad and presented three long versions of the toast which grew out of it, and Labov (1968:69) cites and quotes from others.

The ballad is apparently based on the killing of one Billy Lyon, probably in Memphis around the turn of the century, by an already notorious badman named Lee. The fight or murder is variously explained, but it usually has something to do with Billy's stealing, winning, or spitting on Stack's milkwhite Stetson hat.

In the toast which has evolved from this bully-ballad, the cause of the shooting is usually reduced to the victims' opposition to Stag. Anyone standing up to Stagolee is shot down. In many versions there is a contest between Stag and Billy (or Benny Long, as he is sometimes called), but the issue is seldom more than the question of which of the badmen is badder. In this version, in fact, Stag's motives for killing Billy (whose name has been playfully expanded to Billy Dilly here) seems to be sheer meanness. In most versions Billy at least gets the chance to challenge Stag's status as a badman, but here he barely gets into the room where our hero is taking his woman before he is sexually violated and killed. The sexual coercion is perhaps the supreme proof of Stag's invincible virility.

In all versions, Stag is the victor, and sometimes he triumphs even after his execution for the murder—by bullying the devil into relinquishing the rule of Hell to him.

The version presented here has no such grand dimension. Like the others, it introduces the hero with an ironic description of his reduced circumstances. His "rat-drawn shoes," one of the badges of the Life, are relics of better days. Like Dumbo the Junkie, he doesn't even have the price of a meal. From an epic Southern hero he has become an urban derelict. There is no reference to locale, though the Bucket of Blood bar where, like "Badman Dan," it takes place, is usually identified with New Orleans.

"The Signifying Monkey" and "Stagger Lee" represent opposite ends of the spectrum: the trickster and the badman are seen in these two toasts in their purest forms, motivated by nothing but their mischief and their meanness. Neither is truly a representative type or an object of admiration, but they represent two aspects of the Life's value system in quintessence.

Though both toasts are essentially humorous, the humor in them is different. In the jungle piece there is a certain malicious glee at *la sagesse des petits*, the cunning of the weak; but in "Stagger Lee" there is always a certain irony mixed with the admiration. Stag is a hero but not a model. Like "Death Row" his toast includes a strong element of ridicule. The Life has imposed its urbane and pragmatic angle of vision upon an epic of its forebears.

This version came from Big Stick, a black hustler from upstate New York, in Auburn in 1967. Stick was about twenty and said he had known it for years.

Stagger Lee

Back in '32 when times were hard,
He had a Colt .45 and a deck of cards,

Rat-drawn shoes, an old Stetson hat,
A '28 Ford and payments on that.

His woman threw him out in the ice and the snow
And told him not to come back there no more.

He hadn't copped for a long, long time,
And he had to play with Jojo 'cause he didn't have
                    a dime.

He walked through rain and he walked through mud
Till he came to a place called the Bucket of Blood.   10

He said, "Mr. motherfucker, you must know who I am."
Barkeep said, "No, and I don't give a good goddamn."

He said, "Well, bartender, it's plain to see
I'm that bad motherfucker named Stagger Lee."

Barkeep said, "Yeah, I heard your name down the way,
But I kick motherfucking asses like you every day."

Well, those were the last words the barkeep said,
'Cause Stag put four holes in his motherfucking head.   20

Just then in came a broad named Nellie Brown,
Known to have more coins than any bitch in town.

She came 'cross the bar, pulling up her skirt,
The way the bitch always started to flirt.

She dug the barkeep and said, "He can't be dead."
Stag said, "Well, just count them holes in the
                    motherfucker's head."

She said, "You look like you ain't copped in quite
                    a time.
Why not come to my pad. It won't cost you a dime.

"But there's something I'll have to say before
                    you begin.
You'll have to be gone when Billy Dilly comes in."   30

"I'll stay there till Billy Dilly comes in, till time
                    comes to pass.
And furthermore I'll fuck Billy Dilly in *his*
                    motherfucking ass."

Well, they started to fuck, and she started to fart.
He said, "What's wrong, bitch?" She said, "Coming,
sweetheart."

Just then Billy Dilly rolled in and said, "You must be
That bad motherfucker called Stagger Lee."

"Yeah, I'm Stagger Lee, and you'd better get down on
your knees and slobber my head,
'Cause if you don't, you're sure to be dead."

Billy Dilly dropped down and slobbered on his head,   40
But Stag filled him full of lead.

THE LETTER AND ANSWER TO THE LETTER

Certain toasts, like the four following, are devoted entirely to abuse, a highly developed verbal skill, especially among the young, in the Life.

John Dollard (1939) and Roger D. Abrahams (1962; 1970C:39–60) have written illuminatingly of the verbal contest and shown it to be an elaborated art form among young blacks. Especially refined and stylized is that folk game known as *the dozens*, a verbal contest like the medieval flyting. In playing the dozens, however, two males publicly trade insults. This game has its own conventions, and certain formulaic insults are learned and repeated, but it is essentially a free competition which depends for success on spontaneous oral facility and ingenuity.

Some of the stock abuse of the dozens finds its way into toasts, but its form and object are not the same. The dozens is conventionally played between two males, who direct their abuse to members of each other's families: the typical dozens line contains an obscene reference to the opponent's mother or sister. The insult-toast is also in the form of an exchange, but it is almost always between a man and a woman and contains sexual taunts by one character about the other's mother or sister, as well as direct insults and threats. Typically, the main thrust is at the other's sexual powers or skills. Toasts being a male genre, the man always wins.

Though the two toasts that follow share some features with the relatively childish "Bill and Lil," they have less of a narrative line. They form a unit. The first is never recited alone, but the "Answer" is often quoted, and much of its language has become conventional in the Life. Like most of the literature of abuse, "The Letter" and "Answer to the Letter" form a set rather than a series: an attack and a crushing rejoinder. As in all such exchanges, it is the man who speaks last and best.

The tone of the two is effectively distinguished. The girl's letter is rather a taunt, gloating over her boyfriend's misfortune and goading him with an account of her disloyalty. Only in a few places does she insult him directly: lines 21, 22, and 26 are classical dozens-references, and lines 40, 70–74 are sneers at his sexual prowess and his professional skill respectively. Her object is to hurt him rather than merely to win a verbal contest.

The response, on the other hand, is rich with abuse. Lines 14–16 and 28–32 are a nice blend of signifying and dozens-playing: they make, by indirection, the central statement of the dozens: *I had your mother* (11. 31–32 add her grandmother to his conquests). The rest of the letter is devoted to undermining her confidence and reflecting on her lack of sexual attractions and talents, cleanliness, and skill at the Game.

Unlike "Bill and Lil," this epistolary flyting is truly a contest, a verbal duel in which each goes straight for the vitals with deadly aim.

Lou recited these poems in Attica in 1962. He had heard them both in New York City.

The Letter

I had just come back from Felony Court,
Mad as a motherfucker, with a bad report,

When the door opened and in walked the man,
Carrying what looked like a scribe in his hand.

He said, "Why, what's the matter, son?
You look like you'd shoot me if you had a gun.

"Looks like you're real mad at the whole damned world.
Well, here's a letter from your best girl."

It was a letter from my woman, that much was true,
But that "best girl" stuff just wouldn't do.   10

The letter was postmarked three days old,
So I tore it open before her love turned cold.

"My dearest, darling, adorable one,
You now must pay for the shit you have done.

"You've played the Game, and played it well,
But too much jive has confined you to a cell.

"Yes, cop and blow is the Game, they say,
And I must say I'm glad it turned out this way.

"I went to see your lawyer, but he wasn't in,
So I'll be down to see you, but God knows when.   20

"I went to see your whoring sister, but she was on
                    the roam,
I called your dope fiend brother, but the punk had
                    pawned his phone.

"I bought you some cigarettes and put them on the shelf,
But my habit got the best of me, and I smoked
                    them myself.

"I know you're in there crying you don't like jail,
So get your nasty-ass mammy to go your bail,

" 'Cause if you think this chick's going to bail
                    you free,
Pin this next line and forget about me.

"Remember when you sent me out for coffee and pie?
That's when I called up the F.B.I.   30

"And now I've got you out the way,
Your main man and I can ball every day.

"You remember your main man Red?
Well, he's right beside me in your big brass bed.

"He came by the house just the other night,
Brought some reefer and got my head up tight.

"Then we did it in your best bed.
Why didn't you tell me he was a thoroughbred?

"Yes, we rolled all day, and we rolled all night,
And your main man's loving was out of sight,   40

"Much better than yours, I really must say.
He'd please any woman he sprawled in the hay.

"Oh, Daddy, I slept real good last night,
Knowing you were really up tight.

"You know them clothes you had in pawn?
Well, Red's just your size, and he's got them on.

"And remember that solid gold watch you said cost
                    a grand?
Well, we peeped the back and it said, "Made in
                    motherfucking Japan."[1]

"And as for that money you had hid behind the door—
You ain't slick, motherfucker; it ain't there
                    any more.   50

"I sent you two dollars of it, but don't spend it fast,
'Cause those two bones will be your first and last.

"If you see another bone from this here gal,
St. Peter will call Satan his ace-one pal.

"As far as health goes, I'm all right,
Eating choice food and balling every night.

"I went to see a doctor; he said I need a rest.
So we're taking your short and heading
                    out West.

---

[1]See "Mexicana Rose," 11. 25–26.

"I know you're telling your cellmates you got me
                            up tight,
But I'm sleeping with your main man each and
                            every night.   60

"You can talk all that shit about going upside my head,
But me and your main man are using your bed.

"I know you thought I was cherry, your
                            number-one size,
But I was balling Tony, and you weren't wise.

"I guess you're crying by now—well, that's just
                            too bad.
Face it, sucker, you've just been had.

"Daddy, ain't you hip? My name is Game Nell,
The slickest hooker this side of Hell.

"Quiet as it's kept, I'm a master of the Game,
With tricks from New York to the tip of Spain.   70

"You call yourself a pimp—ain't that a joke!
Every time I saw you, you were always broke.

"Your place is down South, behind a plow,
Except I don't think you could even milk a cow.

"Now I've got your crib, and I've got your short,
And I spoke to the D.A. when I saw him in court.

"So now I know you won't be around,
And Red and I can party all over town.

"Yes, now I know you'll never be free,
And that's the way I planned it to be.   80

"When you get to the pen, look up Green and Blair,
Two more suckers that I sent there.

"Love and kisses from your commonlaw wife.
If you don't get the chair, I hope you get life.

"P.S. Weep, creep."

Answer to the Letter

As I finished her scribe, which was no surprise,
I decided to cut this bitch down to size.

So I pulled out my pencil and opened my pad
And thought, "You don't know it, but *you've* been had."

Then with a smooth quick flip of my hand
Lead touched woodpulp, and *I* began:

"Dear miss adorable tight-cunt bitch,
While reading your letter, I had an itch.

"I got an urge to take a shit
And finished your letter just as I quit.   10

"Paper was scarce, and I had to move fast,
So I used your letter to wipe my ass.

"I'm sorry Red got you and not another,
'Cause in bed you ain't shit compared to your mother.

"She came to see me and left me a dime
And said she'd be back tomorrow some time.

"You talk like I lost something real sweet,
But I got more kick out of beating my meat.

"I'd get more thrill out of popping the dead
Than I got out of you in a nice warm bed.   20

"When I spread your legs, I had to hold my nose;
When you last took a bath, God only knows.

"The hair on your cunt stands up like a steeple,
And you can see crabs walking around like
                    miniature people.

"Every night when I got off your pot,
I went to the doctor for a rabies shot.

"Now as for those threads you took out of pawn,
Don't let your dad catch Red with them on.

"You know that dress I gave you for Christmas you thought
                    was so fly?
Well, I copped that from your mammy last Fourth
                    of July.   30

"And all of your shoes that are under the bed?
They belonged to your grandma, who's long been dead.

"About that money you found behind the door—
What's twenty lousy bones? You think that's a score?

"I'm not worried about the short—you'll have it
                    one more day.
Then the Hertz people be around to tow it away.

"The only thing that I really had
Was my fly crib, a way-out pad.

But, baby, you can forget that too—
'Cause, honey, the mortgage is way overdue.   40

"The only thing I ever gave you was a diamond ring,
And that came from Woolworth, so it ain't worth
                    a thing.

"As for them cigarettes you had on the shelf,
I'm glad you decided to smoke them yourself.

" 'Cause the hacks up this way really know how to swing.
Yeah, baby, in here pot is the thing.

"You'll live high and mighty for a week or so,
But when everything's gone, then where will you go?

"Everyone out there is hip to your game;
You couldn't pull a fast one on a cold-blooded lame.   50

"As to Green and Blair, I hear
They both left the pen sometime last year.

"Al will go back to his main girl Pearl,
And you'll be left alone, little girl.

"Back to the Bowery is where you should go,
'Cause I doubt you'd get a play even on Death Row.

"Well, I didn't get the chair, and life went out too.
My long money banned them—I got one to two.

"Everlasting love from Big Jim Rice.
P.S. Give my regards to your crabs and lice."   60

PIMPING SAM

This sketchy little narrative of the curser outcursed is a rich mix of professional insult, general abuse, and braggadocio. There is more than the dozens here; this is adult stuff. Sam is rejected rather than insulted; Sweet-Loving Nell declines his advances (11. 13–14), threatens him (1. 20), sneers at his appearance (1. 23), and devotes her remaining nineteen lines to boasting of her skills and success in the Life. Sam responds with thirty-seven lines of almost pure boast, much of it conventional in the Life, ranging from sexual swagger to badman threat. Only in lines 64 and 68 does he insult her specifically. Yet like the dozens, this exchange is finally a game; there is no more real hostility between Sweet-Loving Nell and Pimping Sam than between two strangers playing darts in an English pub.

Whether the formulaic boasts of lines 45–52 have entered the vocabulary of the Life from the toast or have been taken from the street and preserved in it can never be certainly known. No doubt both processes occur, as with higher forms of literature.

Jackson (1974:103–108) presents an extended discussion of "Pimping Sam" and its congeners.

This was collected at Clinton Prison in 1955. Many people participated in the recitation, but the official reciter of the toast was Steve, a pimp from New York City who said it was so commonly known among pimps that he could not remember where he first heard it.

Pimping Sam

While sitting here bullshitting with you,
It brings back memories of a bitch I once knew.

While passing through a town out West,
I met this whore who looked like the best.

I was goofing in a bar and feeling real fine,
When in come this whore with a brand-new line.

I was sitting in the corner staring into space,
When she walks to the bar with a heavenly grace.

She was a stomp-down mud-kicker with kelsey hair,
A jive-ass bitch but her face was fair.   10

Now the band started playing, and that was my cue,
So I asked, "May I have this dance with you?"

She turned and gave me a deadly glance
And said, "I'm sorry, but you don't have a chance."

I said, "I didn't mean to step on your toes,
But I thought you was one of them downtown whores.

"A little consolation I thought we might share,
As we lounge around with a few moments to spare."

She said, "A little consolation—there you're right,
'Cause when I'm finished with you, you won't be
                              in sight.   20

"Why, here you are walking the soles off your shoes,
Talking that shit—a little consolation you can use.

"Why, you look as though you've been smoking pot.
Come over to the window and peep what I've got.

"I've got a sky-blue Caddy parked at the curb,
With whisky- and snack-bar all superb."

"You may play damn good cooncan,
But I got all I need to keep my man.

"You think you look slick in them jive-ass clothes,
But you can't bullshit us West Coast whores.   30

"I'm known from the Golden Gate to the coast of Spain,
And the way I beat chumps like you it's a goddamn shame.

"I beat tricks like you every day,
Beat 'em for their clothes, their watches, their pay.

"I'll beat you for your bankroll and your wardrobe, too;
And I'd beat you for your straw, but all suckers
                        don't chew.

"I could take you to my pad and give you the pipe
                        of Gable.
You blink your eyes and I'll have your tongue on
                        my navel.

"And if anyone ask you who put you down,
Tell him Sweet-Loving Nell from across the town."   40

I said, "Hold on, sweetheart, with that jive-ass shit,
'Cause it takes more than that to make a hit.

"I'm Pimping Sam, the biggest in the field,
The man you girls need and the master at the wheel.

"Sometimes I'm known as Ginger Sweet,
Sweet-Dick Daddy, sporting women's treat.

"Pussy-getter, backbone-splitter.
Many a whore holler 'cause it wouldn't fit her.

"Wine-and-whisky-taster, downtown money-waster,
Back-binder, booty-grinder, sweetspot-finder.   50

"Sheet-shaker, cherry-breaker, baby-maker, whores'
                        money taker;
Known to send a whore like you to the undertaker.

"A young whore like you, shaking that thing,
Thinks a man like me is everything.

"Why, listen, bitch, I'll have you know,
I've got French maids to sweep my floor.

"In my pad I've got Chinese cooks
And European whores to read me books.

"I've played east of New York and west of Chi,
And I've got oilwells in Texas your grandaddy
                              couldn't buy.   60

"I'll take a bitch like you who thinks she's smart
And make her shovel shit in a farmer's backyard.

"Next week I'm going to Paris, and I would take you,
But there's nothing in Paris a chump like you could do.

"If it had been the time now like it was in the past,
I'd have been put my Stetsons in your motherfucking ass.

"Why, whore, I'm known from Red Rock to Eagle Pass,
Pulling big-time, rich whores and kicking jive-ass
                    bitches like you in the ass.

"That's me, mackman supreme.
Rich whores cream, poor whores dream.   70

"I'm known to make a bitch swim the Hudson River when
                    it's thirty below,
And dare her ass to shiver when she reaches the
                    motherfucking shore.

"So when you are old and a total wreck,
I hope you fall through your own toilet bowl and break
                    your motherfucking neck.

"And if you have any doubt,
Just tell your friends Pimping Sam was here and just
                    stepped out."

ONE THIN DIME

Abrahams (1970:158–160) offers three versions of this toast as "A Hard-Luck Story" and describes it as "reciting the hardships of being without money." It's true that the little narrative introduction in the first eight lines establishes a point of complaint, as do the opening lines of two of Abrahams' versions; but the essential element seems to lie less in the theme of ingratitude than in the verbal exuberance of the last twelve lines. When this toast is performed, Pete is the hero. The ingenuity of his abuse, gratuitous though it is, gives him the same claim to respect as that of Pimping Sam and the answerer of "The Letter." This abuse-toast happens to be one-sided, but the fun is in the abuse, not necessarily in the competition.

The reference to Korea in the first line of the toast is not particularly significant; it dates only this version. The extravagant demands which make up the bulk of the poem have certainly been around in the Life since before the Korean War. Like Pimping Sam's catalogue of nicknames, they are current specie but have long been negotiable, a fund from which any may draw.

Doe Eye performed this one in Attica in 1962, the contempt in his voice so profound over the last twelve lines it was clear where his sympathies lay.

One Thin Dime

It was wild living in Korea and taking my friends out
                        one at a time,
Giving them beer and whisky and wine.

But when I fell, I fell so fast,
I didn't have a pair of drawers to cover my natural ass.

One day while walking down the street,
I met an old friend, Pimping Pete.

I said, "Hey, Pete, you're looking mighty fine.
How about letting an old friend borrow one thin dime?"

He said, "Before I'd lend you one thin dime, you'd have
                    to cut off both your feet,
Jump off the Empire State Building and go running
                    up the street.   10

"You'd have to catch a she-lion and fuck her in
                    the gutter,
Look up a cow's ass and give me the price of butter.

"You'd have to go to the bottom of the Hudson River and
            bring me back Lena Horn's cunt rag,
Go to the bottom of the East River and bring up dry
                    sand in a bag.

"When your sister's cunt has turned to jelly
And your mother's tits hang down to her belly,

"When the traveling salesman stops fucking the farmer's
                    daughter
And the price of cunt goes down to a quarter,

"Then I'll introduce you to a friend of mine
Who *might* lend you a nickel, but not a motherfucking
                    dime."   20

BOASTS and PRECEPTS

The line between story and non-story is sometimes difficult to draw among toasts; some descriptive or reflective pieces seem to be fragments of stories, and others may be expanded into narratives or incorporated into longer poems already in circulation.

Some non-narrative toasts, however, never were and never will be part of anything else, and among them are to be found some of the best-known pieces in the repertoire.

The seven non-narrative toasts given here fall into two groups, boasts and precepts.

Most popular among the young, boasts give us a good idea of what the Life respects or values in its members. All are spoken by players, and all are characterized by swagger, but they vary widely in tone and emphasis. The first speaker is a pimp who rejoices in his expertise, the second a pimp who glories in his power, and the third a gloating thief—closer to the white tradition of large-scale crime than to the cunning of the Life.

A few toasts, neither narratives nor boasts, state the values of the Life directly. "The Pool-Shooting Monkey" ends with an explicit moral, but some toasts are purely didactic or cautionary. Apparently prompted by the preceptorial spirit,

152

such toasts are directed rather to the apprentice than to the player. They offer advice and warning to the novice and afford him a manual of the world he is entering. Nothing in the corpus provides so clear and direct a view of the dynamics of the Life as these tutelary verses.

MASTER OF THE LONG-SHOE GAME

A particularly pure example of the boast, "Master of the
Long-Shoe Game" shows no evidence of being a fragment of a
longer piece. The long-shoe game of the title—another term
for pimping, although often used for the Life itself—is mentioned in "Broadway Sam" (1. 8) and "Honky-Tonk Bud" (1.
108), and it is his status as a pimp which gives Long-Shoe
Sam, the narrator of "Mexicana Rose," his nickname. The
reference is to the favored shoe-style among pimps in the
1940's and 1950's, the narrow, pointed-toe Oxford—a part of
the uniform of the Life.

The five personages named in lines 13–16 are familiar from
other toasts. Long-Shoe Sam and Smitty Cocaine are the
traveling pimps in "Mexicana Rose." Duriella du Fontaine,
who here sacrifices the particle in her name to the scansion,
has her own toast, as does Honky-Tonk Bud. Bad Dan may be
either the Badman Dan who is killed by Two-Gun Green or the
Bad Dan who kills Billy Clapshit, but neither of these badmen
really belongs in this list of pimps. The John Ford in line 23 is
presumably a slip of the tongue for Henry.

Jim, who recited this in Clinton in 1955, was a ditty
bopper—a youngster whose pretensions to success in the Life
no one believed. He delivered the toast as though it applied to
himself, but he did not claim to have invented it; he said,
rather, that he had learned it from another young black in New
York but that he understood it was an old, established toast.

Master of the Long-Shoe Game

Now if you ask me what's my fame,
I am the Master of the Long-Shoe Game.

When they see me coming, young hustlers hide,
Pimps lose their pride, prostitutes side.

When you tell me about the mack,
You've got to run it down fact by fact.

For any old story don't unfold—
I've heard every story that's ever been told.

I'm a young girl's pleasure, an old woman's treasure,
Known to be the world's best dresser.   10

Here's some dudes I've taught the game;
Maybe you'll know them as I call them by name:

Long-Shoe Sam and Smitty Cocaine
And the man who pulled Duriella Fontaine,

Big Bad Dan and another stud,
A sharp young slicker named Honky-Tonk Bud.

My proclamation is to whores' dope fiends,
To two-bit chislers and mack men supreme,
To rich tricks who pay whores to fulfill their dreams.

To all of you who think you're slick,   20
Sit down and listen while I shoot my stick:

I own forty-five golden Cadillacs,
Got more dough than John Ford and Rockefeller back
                              to back.

Now I ask all of you to praise my name,
For I am the Master of the Long-Shoe Game.

THE HUSTLER

"The Hustler" is spoken in a vaunting style by a con man (1. 1) and pimp (1. 2) who sounds more like Stagger Lee than like Honky-Tonk Bud. The references in lines 6 and 7 place the composition of at least those lines between the accession of Pope Paul in 1964 and the death of Robert Kennedy in 1968; line 10, in which the fighter is called Cassius rather than Muhammed, must have been composed soon after the Clay-Liston fight of 1964. But toasts are as hospitable to new lines as they are amenable to the loss of old, and those noted might well have supplanted others with references to earlier personages, as line 13 suggests.

It was heard, in fact, in 1966, probably soon after its composition, from Boxcar in Auburn. He had been in prison for only a short time and said that he had learned it from "the guys" in Jersey City.

The Hustler

The name of the game is beat the lame,
Take a woman and make her live in shame.

It makes no difference how much she scream or holler,
'Cause dope is my heaven and my God the
                              almighty dollar.

I, the Hustler, swear by God
I would kill Pope Paul if pressed too hard,

I would squash out Bobby and do Jackie harm
And for one goddamn dollar would break her arm.

I, the Hustler, kick ass morning, noon, and night,
I would challenge Cassius and Liston to a fight.   10

I would climb in the ring with nothing but two P-.38's
And send either one that moved through the
                    pearly gates.

I, the Hustler, can make Astaire dance and
                    Sinatra croon,
And I would make the Supreme Court eat shit from
                    a spoon.

DO YOU KNOW WHAT IT MEANS?

This taunt is spoken by a criminal to his victim. It is implicit here that the speaker has been acquitted, if he has been caught, and can thus afford to boast.

"Do You Know What It Means?" has a couple of references outside the Life: reservations at Sardi's and the submission of "the mob" seem related to organized crime. But this toast contains nearly every status symbol of the Life as well: Fleetwood Cadillacs, narcotics, expensive clothes, and power to impress novice hustlers are all classic goals in the community. The two-hundred-dollar suits and forty-dollar hats place the first line before 1970 or so, but the importance of blacks in organized crime was not sufficient at that time to support such a fantasy. It may be that this poem is a white verse adapted into the Life.

This toast was heard from whites as frequently as from blacks, but the former recognized it as black. This version was delivered by Slim in Auburn in 1966.

Do You Know What It Means?

Do you know what it means to wear two-hundred-dollar
suits and forty-dollar hats,
To drive through the streets in Fleetwood Cadillacs?

Do you know what it means to have a supply of C and
a supply of horse,
Not to need any connections because you're the
big boss?

Do you know what it means to wear silk shirts on your
back and hundred-dollar shoes on your feet,
To have more people working for you than there are
faggots on Forty Second Street?

Do you now what it means to give every young
                    hustler a break,
To fill his pockets with money and his stomach
                    with steak?

Do you know what it means to keep your women in mink
                    and sable
And have Sardi's in New York reserve you a table?   10

Do you know what it means to have the mob call you
                    King and the cops call you Mister,
To have the D.A. offer his mother and the judge put up
                    his sister?

Do you know what it means? No, you never could know
                    what it means, and you never will,
'Cause you're one of the chumps who pay my bill.

SPORTING LIFE

A serene and sagacious catalogue of the delights and demands of the Life, this poem devotes 14 stanzas to activities and characters and the remaining 6 to advice on how to succeed. Addressed to the neophyte, it enjoins ingenuity, obduracy, courage, and patience as the dues he must pay for the pleasures the Life promises. The tone is that of master to apprentice.

Both the title—the term was obsolescent by the late 1930's—and the emphasis on confidence trickery and petty theft are evidence of the relative antiquity of "Sporting Life," but its spirit is ageless.

Pop, in Auburn, regarded this toast as the best he knew, and it clearly evoked great nostalgia for him. His recitation of it in 1967 stimulated lively discussion and general agreement on its truth to life.

Sporting Life

There are big hotels with sultry belles
    Strung all along the lobby.
Yes, there's a lass from every class,
    And night life is her hobby.

There are painted lips and swaying hips
    And makeup patted on.
The country hick and the city trick
    Are the suckers that are drawn.

There are diamonds shining while couples are dining,
    Sipping cocktails for two,   10
And life appears in silver tears,
    And your blues are not so blue.

Where life occurs with ermine furs
    That a girl may win with a smile,
A rosy cheek on a bed that squeaks
    Is most definitely in style.

There are long trips on luxury ships
    To many a distant port;
Some Cuban rum, some Latin fun,
    And gambling just for sport.   20

But just let me say, it's the dues you pay
    In order to live like this.
You can't just dream, you've got to scheme;
    You really must have a twist.

So from a square you depart and cheer up your heart
    In order to succeed,
But for a better start, you cut out your heart
    'Cause it's an organ you really don't need.

You forget the quote that the Christians wrote
    About honesty and fair play,   30
For you can't live sweet not knowing how to cheat;
    The Game don't play that way.

There are old con men in some smoky den,
    Scheming on some lame.
They seldom lose, for they travel in twos
    And vice a chump in the game.

There's the blow-up bang and the paper-hang
    Where some poor chump gets beat.
There are two-way layers and old stuff players,
    And all know how to cheat.   40

There's the dude on the stoop dealing in hot loot
    To many an eager one,
And the the tough torpedo in the silk tuxedo,
    Proving his way with a gun.

There are fellows who laugh when they use the gaff
    To take a sucker's dough.
They drop their bait in every state,
    And they're always on the go.

There are teen-age hipsters and bull-dagging sisters,
    All mixed up in one bowl,   50
Hustling vipers and pocketbook swipers
    All aiming at their goal.

There are faggots in drag and hookers in rags,
    Out to turn a trick,
There are Miss Murphy walkers—oh, they're convincing
                talkers—
    Yes, everyone wants to be slick.

There's the neighborhood cop at the numbers drop,
    Shaking down the run,
But he may lose his grand to a stickup man
    At the point of a blue steel gun.   60

There's the cool old shot at the busy bus stop
    Scanning on a hide.
The crowds all crush in the afternoon rush
    When the squares all take their ride.

There are junkies with habits who run like rabbits
    Whenever they see the man,
And slick dope sellers who deal with those fellows
    And retire as soon as they can.

Yes, life is sweet when lived on the street.
    All you need is heart.   70
A bag of stuff is more than enough
    To give a man his start.

But though your stomach may gripe on some
                      sleepless night
    As you're climbing the ladder
With holes in your shoes—that's paying your dues,
    And it really doesn't matter.

Just bear in mind that you must do time
    Whenever you pull a bone.
So don't cry in terror when you make an error—
    Just do your bid and go home.   80

DO YOUR CRYING FOR THE LIVING

This toast contrasts significantly with "Sporting Life"; they have the same preceptorial intent but different angles of vision. The speaker here is also a professional advising a tyro, but his advice is grim: instead of a garden of earthly delights which, with diligence, his pupil can enjoy, the Life has become a darkling plain. A fundamental difference of temperament distinguishes the two speakers.

There is also a difference of era. "Do Your Crying" deals with the Life of the 1950's and 60's and reflects the change which it had undergone since the sporting life of the 30's and 40's. The Life has lost its joyous diversity; pimping is the Game now. In the earlier poem, life was sweet when lived on the street—if you had the heart (or lack of heart) for it. In "Do Your Crying," it has become a "steady grind," as the narrator of "The Fall" calls it. The steel has entered its soul. Patience and determination are no longer enough; violence and cruelty are necessary just to keep the hustler out of Father Divine's.

"Do Your Crying for the Living" was often quoted, seldom recited complete; the opening line was proverbial in the Life. This version, the longest encountered, was delivered by Duke in Auburn in 1964.

Do Your Crying for the Living

Do your crying for the living, hustling their butter
                    and lard,
'Cause dying comes easy, but it's the living
                    that's hard.

It's an everyday grind for that rice and grits,
A constant watch for that number that never hits.

From the crack of dawn till the setting sun,
If you're a hustler, my man, your work's just begun.

You wake up in the morning—that is, if you've been
         to bed—
Wondering where did you get such a miserable
         fucked-up head.

You stare in the mirror to see just how you stand,
Forgetting you went broke last night dealing with the
         heroin man.   10

On your table's your bankroll—just two dimes and a penny.
Father Divine may not be God, but his cheap meals sure
         saved a many.

Say you cop a choice chick and you're really doing great,
The scratch is right and the set up looks straight.

Yes, you've walked around chickless for many a moon,
But after you pulled the first one, all the other
         whores swooned.

They're standing in line and don't mind waiting,
Because you're one of the sharpest dudes ever stepped out
         of Layton.

Now you're playing real hard, hard as a rock—
But look out, brother, you're in for a shock.   20

Your broad becomes lazy, trifling and slack,
And starts signifying about your not having a license
         to mack,

About the weather being bad and the business
         being slow,
And the bluecoat on the beat taking all her dough.

Well, I can tell you, friend, your woman's just lying,
'Cause there's some good C downtown, and your bitch
         is buying.

You probably think it's some other dude who's handsome
                              and tall,
But it's a little jasper broad, and she's cute and small.

Now I know you don't go for a lot of flings
Like sucking her pussy and all of those things,   30

But I can tell you, in the street they got pimps
Who'll suck your broad's pussy till her heart contents.

So my advice to you is get on the ball,
Bow your head, and that ain't all.

Put your ass on her shoulder and knock that bitch down,
Keep your foot in her ass till the snow hits the ground.

Make her straighten up and walk a chalk line,
Or you'll be eating *your* next meal at Father Divine.

KING HEROIN

"King Heroin" is the most familiar of all junkie toasts. Like its subject, it cuts across race and class and may be heard in prison and poolhall, home and hallway.

The first version, by far the most common, has nothing distinctively black about it, but it has a firm place in the toast literature. The violent imagery of this dramatic personification exerts a powerful grip on the imagination in the Life, and many of its lines have passed into the proverbial wisdom of the community.

"The pleasure of kings" here becomes a king itself, but an evil, destructive one. "King Heroin" is not alone in condemning narcotics, whose victims include many toast heroes, but its comminatory intention sets it apart.

Agar (1971:183–184) points out the contrast between the images of the addict in "King Heroin" and in "Honky-Tonk Bud"; the hipcat stud is an admired member of his community, though an addict, but "King Heroin" speaks to his "victims" and, in the spirit of the badman boast, glories in his power to destroy them. Where "Sporting Life" gently reminds the beginner of the pitfalls and demands of the Life and "Do Your Crying" grimly outlines the difficulties of pimping, "King Heroin" issues the ultimate warning.

Of the many recitations of "King Heroin" heard, Super-junkie's in Clinton in 1955 was both the most complete and the most dramatic. At the last line his voice faded away to a ghostly rasp that sent chills down the spines of his listeners.

King Heroin

Behold, my friend,
I am Heroin, known to all as the killer of men.

Where I come from no one knows.
I come from the land where the poppy grows.

I came to this country without a passport,
And ever since then I've been hunted and sought.

Whole nations have gathered to plot my destruction,
For I am the breeder of crime and corruption.

My little white grains are nothing but waste.
I am soft, deadly, and bitter to taste.   10

I am seldom pure, often diluted,
And once in your blood, I'll make it polluted.

I'll stand on my record; I'll make all men
Who dare to use me wallow in sin.

I'll take the gold from a rich man and make him poor,
Take a foolish virgin and make her a whore,

Make a husband forsake his wife,
Send a greedy man to jail for life.

I'll make a schoolboy forget his books,
Make a famous beauty forget her looks.   20

In a glassine bag I find my way
To gentlemen in offices and children at play,

To heads of state, to the lowest bum,
To the richest estate or the poorest slum.

But regardless of position or reason for use,
Once in your blood, I'll give but abuse.

To some I'm joy, adventure, a thriller;
I put a gun in their hands and make them a killer.

To some I'm salvation, to others a must,
But I make their souls grow heavy with lust.   30

Those who use me more than most,
I kill them off with an overdose.

Do you want to hear more of the things I do?
The women I defiled, the men I slew?

In China I stopped an army to the very last man,
I'm honored in Turkey, respected in Japan.

Oh, I am a great god to behold,
More precious than diamonds, more treasured than gold.

More potent than whisky, more deadly than wine,
For I am the scourge of all mankind.   40

To keep up your habit, you do your best.
You work and steal until your arrest.

With cramps in your stomach you vomit and cough,
Till in days of this madness you may throw me off.

You curse my name, defy me in speech,
But you use me again if I am in reach.

And after the rush comes, you don't think me mean;
You praise my name and nod off to dream.

So run if you want to. I won't even chase.
I'll be at the gate when you come for your taste.   50

You heard my warning and didn't take heed,
So put your foot in the stirrup and mount the steed.

Get tight in the saddle and ride it well,
For I'm the white horse that will take you to Hell.

KING HEROIN II

The wide circulation of "King Heroin" has led to many variants. The one given below departs from the original so far as to be virtually a new toast.

Except for the opening lines and the spirit of the piece, it has little in common with its model. Its point of view veers wildly from that of the drug itself (11. 1–4, 7–8) to those of a dealer (11. 5–6, 19–20), an outside observer (11. 9–18), and, finally, an addict (11. 21–32). Though essentially descriptive, it contains none of the imagery which characterizes the original and none of its elevated language. Several usages—including the word "toast" in the penultimate line—identify it as being of black origin.

But the many stylistic differences between these two versions of "King Heroin" do not affect their fundamental kinship: both the dramatic monologue with its sustained personification and the wandering doggerel which derives from it are, in essence, urgent warnings to the uninitiated of the dangers of narcotics.

Among the corrections and sequels volunteered after Superjunkie's performance of "King Heroin," Jim's version seemed most distinct, and the group agreed it was another toast.

King Heroin II

Look now, my friends, for I am here;
My name is Heroin, and I am very near.

You can buy me here, you can buy me there,
You can buy me almost anywhere.

If you think life's a drag,
Give me three dollars, and I'll sell you a bag.[1]

---

[1]Old price for a minimum dose of heroin. It is to this classic three-dollar bag that the narrator of "Kitty Barrett" refers in line 23.

Just cook me up when you're good and ready,
And you won't remember if you're Johnnie or Eddie.

But here's the bad part—it's about the man.
If he catches you, you go to the can.   10

He'll punch you, kick you, knock you to the dust,
'Cause there's nothing he likes better than a junkie bust.

And when you're sick and start in crying,
He won't give a fuck if you're living or dying.

Your arms will be withered and black as the night,
Your eyes still watering from when you were up tight.

This drug ain't like whisky or a bottle of wine;
If you don't watch it, it'll go to your mind.

Then you are hooked on this drug of mine,
And to get it you'll commit any kind of crime.   20

Oh, God, my days on this earth are short,
And then I'll be going to your heavenly court.

Judge me with pity and fairness alike,
For I fucked up my days on earth with a spike,

With cotton and tweezers and bottle cap, too.²
God, I didn't mean it, but I even cursed you.

And when my day of reckoning is near,
Please get the junkie who should really be here.

He gave me my wings, that dirty rat fuck—
He thought he was slick, only charging a buck.   30

Well, now this toast has got to stop.
You want to know why? 'Cause I got to cop.

²Part of "the works"—the addict's equipment. The bottle cap—or a spoon—is for cooking up heroin, the cotton for drawing up and filtering the solution, and the tweezers for handling the cotton.

Glossary
AND
Bibliography

Glossary

The following list attempts to provide definitions for words or phrases which may be obscure in toasts; it does not pretend to be a comprehensive lexicon of the Life. Many of the entries have wide currency in different senses, and others have dropped out of use altogether except for their scarcely understood repetition in toasts.

The language of these verses is that of one segment of the urban black lower class, but no sharp line can be drawn around such a vocabulary. Much white underworld slang has found a place in it, and much of it has moved the other way into the speech of the white underworld, the white drug scene, the music world, and, more recently, the youth culture. No effort has been made to label black, prison, criminal, or youthful usage except where there is an absolute restriction to such vocabularies, since such discrimination would now be unrealistic; neither prison, the Life, nor the wider black community is so isolated that the vocabulary of each can be clearly delimited.

175

A note has been made in brackets before each definition here of the entry's appearance in any of five references: *Dictionary of American Slang* (1960) by Harold Wentworth and Stuart Berg Flexner—"W&F"; the revised second edition with supplement of that book—"W&F²"; *Dictionary of Afro-American Slang* (1970) by Clarence Major—"M"; *The Third Ear: A Black Glossary* (1971) by Hermese E. Roberts— "R"; and *Black Jargon in White America* (1972) by David Claerbut—"C." Where no bracketed initial follows the part-of-speech label, the entry or particular sense of the entry employed in the toast cited appears in none of these dictionaries. Appearance in other sources is noted where that fact seems useful.

Following each definition there is a list of the exact locations of the entry in the toasts. These have been given by title and line, the abbreviated titles listed alphabetically. The following abbreviations have been used for the titles of the toasts:

Glossary

ace *adj* [W&F, R] Best, main (MR69)

ace-one See ACE (L54)

all *adv* Completely, very (contemptuous) (F211; MR74)

ass *n* 1: [M] Self, person (with possessive, by synecdoche) (F216; PS73; PSM22; SM12, 18, 28, 36, 53, 56, 60, 73, 74, 76; 2SM10, 16)   2: Courage, skill, capacity (esp. in fighting) (2SM40, 42)

ass, be [someone's] *v phr* Be the end (for someone; always in "It [that] is [was, etc.] [someone's] ass") (GDW89)

-ass [M as "assed"] An intensive suffix for adjectives (F85; L26; PS10, 29, 41, 68; SM6; 2SM6)

bad *adj* 1: [W&F, M, C, R] Good, brave, powerful, independent (This curious transposition of values has been widely noted, perhaps in greatest depth by Brearly [1939] and by Dundes [1973:578 – 579, 580–581] in his introduction to Brearly.) (BMD10, 38, 42, 62, 70, 76, 80; BSm12; RHTB73; SM42; 2SM26; SLee16, 36) 2: Arrogant, presumptuous (SM6; 2SM41)

bag n [W&F²] Container of narcotics, esp. heroin, which is often sold in glassine or plastic bags; hence, a supply of narcotics (GDW161; 2HK6; HTB23, 55; SL71)

ball vi [W&F, M] Engage in sexual intercourse (L32, 56)   vt Engage in sexual intercourse with (L64)

beast n Habit, esp. narcotics addiction (cf. *monkey on* [one's] *back*) (BSm48)

beat vt [R] Rob from (KB16; H1)

beat (for) adj in need (of); eager (for) (MR68)

benny n [W&F] man's overcoat (PSM14)

bid n Variant of ʙɪᴛ (possibly reinforced by sense of *bidding*) (SL80)

Big Apple, the [W&F, M] New York City (MR73)

big bucks n pl A large sum of money (DdF180; GDW114)

bill n [W&F] One hundred dollars (KB34; RHTB147)

bit n 1: [W&F, M] Prison sentence (WE39)   2: [M] Rôle, life style (F206)

bitch n Woman (not pejorative) (BMD56; F96, 100, 111, 112, 120, 183, 189, 193, 197, 100; DdF90, 100, 195, 200; KB21; MR51, 67, 97, 132; SM50)

blow vi 1:[W&F] Smoke (marijuana) (F150)—**blow on** vt Inhale (narcotics) (MR85)   2: vi, vt [W&F, M] Fail, lose, exhaust (F151, 153, 205, 207, 222; GDW55, 71, 123, 128; L17; MR116)   3: vt Spend (GDW139)

bluecoat n [W&F²] Policeman (DYC25; WE8 attrib)

blues n pl Money (from *blue chips*) (BD6)

boat n Prison transfer (New York prison use) (HTB132)

bone n Dollar (AL34; L52, 53)

book vt Destine (BD7 p. part)

boost vi, vt [W&F] Shoplift (F78)

booster [W&F] Shoplifter (HTB38; SH12)

booty n [R] See ʀᴏᴜɴᴅ-ᴇʏᴇ (black use) (PS50)

boss adj [W&F, M, C, R] Excellent, the best (BSm35; DJ33; DdF20, 42, 153; GDF7; KB8, 23; KM87; MR99; RHTB13, 247)

bread n [W&F, M, C, R] Money (BMD30; F119, 207, 220; DdF40, 116; HTB35, 117, 121; PSM35; RHTB70)

break vt Tip brim (of a hat) at a rakish angle (GDW11)

buck the saw v phr Go against impossible odds (F128)

bull-dag vi Practice lesbianism (back formation from *bull-dagger*, variant of *bull-diker*, *bull-dike* 'lesbian') (SL49 pres. part.)

bust n Arrest (2HK12; HTB67, 70) vt [M, C, R] Arrest (KB47)

bust [someone's] **ass** v phr Beat severely (*bust* 'strike, break' + ᴀss) (BL8)

bust [one's] **nuts** *v phr* [M] Have an orgasm, ejaculate (F123)

C *n* [W&F, M] Cocaine (DdF81; DYK3; DYC26; MR129)

can *vt* [W&F] Stifle (DR78)

canned heat *n* Alcohol-based fuel manufactured to heat food but drunk by alcoholics (F23)

cap *n* 1: Bullet (DR38; MR156)   2: [W&F] Term of address to person in authority (RHTB306)   3: See HEAD (F117)

cherry *n* [W&F] Virgin (L63)

chew *vi* Be gullible, *take the bait* (PS36)

choked up (tight) *adj* Formally dressed (of a man, referring to buttoned shirt collar) (HTB5)

chump *n* Person (not necessarily stupid) (HTB33)

clean *adj* [C, R] Elegantly dressed, PRESSED, FLY (GDW3; MR12; PSM10)

cold-blooded *adj* See STONE, (probably from such expressions as *cold-blooded murder*; here only an intensive) (DdF39)

come *n* [W&F] Semen (from verb *come* 'have an orgasm, ejaculate') (BF71, 81)

come down *vi* Be disclosed (of a HAND) (F78)

come down front *vi* Expose oneself, tell the truth about oneself (GDW155)

come on *vi* [W&E] Present oneself, appear (with adjective) (GDW75, 98)

come up weak *vi* Disappoint expectations (MR93)

commissary *n* Prison shop where inmate may buy food, toilet articles, etc. (BL6)

cook up *vi, vt* Prepare (heroin) for injection by dissolving in water over heat (2KH7)

cool *n* [W&F] Composure (with keep, lose, BLOW) (DR54)

coon *vt* Beat at cooncan (PSM54, 58, 61, 62)

cooncan *n* Rummy game popular among blacks (Supposed to be from Spanish *con quien* 'with whom' [see Abrahams, 1970:259], but possibly from Greek *koumkan* 'rummy,' a similar Greek card game; though there has been more contact between United States blacks and Spanish-speaking people than between blacks and Greeks, the fact that COONCAN is never played with partners suggests that the derivation of the name from *con quien* is a folk etymology.) (BSk4, 8 [nickname]; PS27)

cop *vi* [W&F²] Obtain something (usually illegal or improper, such as narcotics or sex; hence, have sexual relations) (F222; GDW128, 148, 162; 2KH32; HTB29; KB12; L17; RHTB173, 214;

SM51; SLee7, 27)   *vt* [W&F², M, R] Obtain, receive (AL30; BF77; DdF5, 72; DYC13; F105, 225; HTB44, 137; MR123; RHTB36, 49)

cop and blow A formulaic expression of the vicissitudes of fortune. Equivalent to: "You win some, you lose some"; "Everyone has his ups and downs." (F222; GDW128; L17)

cop a plea *v phr* [W&F] Plead guilty to a (usually lesser) charge offered by the prosecution; hence (uncited), make excuses (DR13)

cop out *vi* [W&F] See COP A PLEA. (Though the original meaning continues to serve its specialized purpose, it is losing currency because of the widespread use of the term with the derived sense 'be evasive, offer excuses.' Indeed, M and C give only the latter definition.) (GDW51)

crack for *vt* Request (DR23)

cream *vi* Have an orgasm, ejaculate (PS70)

crib *n* [W&F, M, C, R] See PAD (originally 'bed,' hence place to sleep) (AL28; L75)

cross, in a See IN A CROSS

crown *n* See LID (HTB8)

cut loose *vt* [M] Break off relations with (DR32)

daddy *n* Woman's term of address to a lover, PAPA (F104; GDW120; KB29, 45; L43, 67)

deal in zeros *v phr* Fail completely (KM137)

dig *vi, vt* [W&F, C, R] 1: Notice, listen to, watch, PIN (DdF79; GDE15; HTB2, 10, 11, 16, 20, 57, 60, 98; KB14, 36; KM2, 102, 106, MR84,135, 136; RHTB232; SM27)   2: Understand (KM36, HTB150)

dig [oneself] *v phr* Realize one's position or limitations, get wise to oneself (DR54)

dike, dyke *n* [W&F, C] Lesbian (HTB90)

dime *n* 1: [C] Ten dollars (sometimes *big dime*, distinguished from *change dime*) (AL15)   2: [W&F², M] Ten-year prison sentence (KM92)

ditty bop, ditty bopper *n* [W&F, M] Immature person, adolescent, esp. one pretending to be sophisticated or one who makes a display (contemptuous) (SM20; WE7)

do *vt* Serve (of a prison sentence) (BF97; GDW57; SL77)

down *adj* 1: [W&F², M, C] Aware, sophisticated, successful (possibly from DOWNTOWN) (DdF24, 33, 197; GDW122; HTB6; KB17); stylish (MR16) 2: Low (of a supply) (HTB29)

down front, come See COME DOWN FRONT

downtown *adj* Living or operating outside of Harlem, which is in upper Manhattan; hence, high-class, successful (PS16, 49)

drag *n* [W&F] Transvestitism —**in drag** *adj* Wearing the clothes of the opposite sex (BSM59; HTB99) —**play drag** Solicit customers while dressed in the clothes of the opposite sex (of a prostitute) (F76)

drop [one's] **drawers** *v phr* submit sexually (BMD58)

dude *n* [R] Man (BF50; DR30; DYC18, 27; MLSG11; RHTB273; SL41)

eighth *n* One-eighth ounce of narcotics, esp. heroin, ordinarily diluted to about 2 percent strength. (David W. Maurer [1971] suggests also "about one gram or approximately 60 grains of . . . morphine," and Richard R. Lingeman [1969] further identifies an eighth as "a rough measure for the purpose of sale") (DJ41)

fall *n* Arrest and conviction (F title, 272; WE2)   *vi* [W&F] Be arrested and convicted (F5)

find a stump to fit [one's] **rump** *v phr* Sit down, make oneself comfortable (PSM25)

firing *adj* Eager, ready (F217)

flag, flag down *vt* Arrest (RHTB54; HTB138)

flat *adj* [W&F] Without money (HTB43)

fly *adj* [C, R] See CLEAN (AL29, 38; DdF5, 69, 123; GDW11, 119; KB7; KM27)

foxy *adj* Beautiful (of a woman, from *fox* 'beautiful woman') (SH9)

frail *n* [W&F] Woman (F214)

freak *n* [M] Person with deviate sexual taste (not pejorative) (BF title, 40, 53, 97; DdF20)

freakish, freaky *adj* Sexy (DJ32)

freak off *vi* Engage in deviate sexual activity (BF20)

from the start *adj phr* As the minimum term of an indeterminate prison sentence (GDW53)

front *n* [W&F, M] Man's suit (HTB6)

fry *vt* [W&F] Electrocute (DR1)

funk *n* Smegma, semen; hence filth (BF87) —**funky** *adj* [R as "smelly"] Filthy (BSm58)

funny-time *adj* Odd, ridiculous, disreputable (HTB13; MR72)

gaff *n* [W&F] Trick, hoax (originally a device in carnival betting game which controlled the outcome; whence *blow the gaff* 'reveal the trick') (SL45)

game n 1: Particular activity in the Life, shady or criminal business, swindle (F59, 91, 147; DdF106; GDW64; MLSG title, 2, 25; SH15)   2: Business or property (not necessarily in the Life) (DdF198)   3: Skill in the activities of the Life (usually with possessive) (MR78, 106)   vi Engage in the activities of the Life, PLAY (F48)

Game, the n The Life, SPORTING LIFE (BF8; F3, 10, 116, 193, 221, 271; BSm79; DdF198; GDW64, 192; HTB80, 149; KM53; L15, 17, 67 [nickname], 69; MLSG11; MR71, 95; RHTB94; SL36)

gat n [W&F, M] Gun (probably from Gatling gun) (BS21)

gee n Collar, often improvised of paper, used to fasten needle into eye-dropper when injecting narcotics (HTB50)

get down (heavy) vi Play for (high) stakes, bet (heavily) (BSk11)

get in the wind [R] vi Leave (GDW127)

get on vi Become elevated, enter into a narcotic state (HTB48)

gig n 1: [W&F, C] Party (BF11) 2: See STING (GDW160)

gin vi Engage in sexual intercourse (of a woman, possibly related to *gin* [n and vi] 'fight') (F164)

give [someone] **his hat** v phr Release from prison (KB48)

give [someone] **his wings** v phr Introduce to narcotics, give or sell narcotics to, *turn on* (2KH29)

go [someone's] **bail** v phr Provide bail bond for (F55)

go down vi Happen, occur (BSm65)

good-doing adj Successful, doing well (DdF7; GDW title, passim [nickname]; KB31; RHTB16)

greasy [grizi] adj Dirty, shabby, slovenly (sometimes distinguished from [grisi] 'covered with grease') (DR12 [nickname]; GDW149, 150)

green door n Door leading into the execution chamber of a prison (New York prison use) (DR61)

guebe [gibi, gubi] **dust** n Powder believed to have magic properties (Probably from *goober* [from Kongo *nguba*] 'peanut,' usually one of its ingredients, but Jackson [personal communication] suggests that it "may be related to 'goofer dust,' powder used in various conjure techniques and known throughout the rural South and much of the urban North where there have been large black in-migrations. In some accounts, it comes from the bone of a black cat caught in a graveyard on the night of the new moon.") (BF90)

hack n [W&F, M] Prison guard (AL45; DR23, 28, 68, 87; RHTB176, 309; SH38)

hand n Capacity, ability, power (from *hand* 'cards held in a round of play') (F78)

hard as lard adj Soft, refined; hence skillful (PSM23)

head n 1: Oral sex, CAP, LID (BMD25, 29, 32; DdF96; F119, 173) 2: [W&F] Glans of the penis (DdF96; SLee37, 40) 3: State of mind, mental condition (DdF103)

hemp n [W&F] See HERB (MR85)

herb n [C, R] Marijuana (PSM17)

hide n [W&F] Wallet, POKE (SL62)

hip to adj Aware of (AL49; F213; RHTB47)

hit vi Use narcotics (F150)

hit on vt [W&F, M] Make (usually sexual) advances to (MR66, 75)

hole card n Hidden truth about someone (from game of blackjack) (MR72)

hooker n Prostitute (L68; SL53)

horn, around the, take v phr Kiss or lick (someone's) entire body, *tongue-wash, take around the world* (F70)

horse n [W&F, M] Heroin (DYK3)

hustle vi [R] Engage in the activities of the Life, GAME, PLAY (DJ22, 23; DdF124, 148; MR121; SL51) vt Get with difficulty (DYC1)

hustler n Participant in the Life, PLAYER (DYK7; DYC6; H title, 5, 9, 13; DJ20; KM77, 137; MLSG3; MR133)

hype n [W&F] Hypodermic syringe; eye-dropper used as syringe (HTB49)

ice n [W&F] Jewelry (F155) vt [W&F²] Kill, PUT ON ICE (DR39)

in a cross adv In a difficult position, in trouble, IN A SLING (F178; MR100)

in a sling adv See IN A CROSS (WE9)

Jack n [R] See JIM (KB28)

jasper n [M] Female homosexual (BF21; DYC28; F69; KM129)

jean n Female customer of a prostitute (from JOHN) (F71)

Jim n [M, C, R] Term of address to male (equivalent to white *Mac*) (MR12; WE21)

jive n Frivolity, foolishness (L116; SM38) vi [W&F, M, C, R] Talk idly, frivolously, insincerely (RHTB73) adj [C] Trivial, foolish, insignificant, absurd (BMD82; PS10, 29, 41, 68; PSM26)

john n Male customer of a prostitute (F71)

johnnie n [W&F] See JOHN; respectable man (BMD6)

Jojo n Personification of the penis (SL338)

juicy *adj* Sexy (of a woman) (HTB89) favorable (of conditions) (SH23)

juke *adj* Cheap, sleazy (of a saloon, probably from *jukebox*) (F85)

keep [one's] **feet in** [one's] **pants** *v phr* stay quiet, be careful, stay in one place, *play close to the chest* (KM4, 108)

keep (have) [one's] **feet in** [someone's] **pocket** *v phr* Harass, hound (KM61)

kelsey *n* Straight hair style formerly popular among black prostitutes (from *kelsey* 'prostitute') (PS9 attrib)

kick *vi* [M] Overcome (esp. a narcotics habit) (BF82)

kick mud *v phr* Work as a prostitute, esp. in the street (F194) —**mud-kicker** *n* Prostitute, streetwalker (PS9)

kicks *n* [W&F, M, C, R] Shoes (BSm10)

kiester (also **keister, keester**) *n* [W&F, M] Buttocks (DR50; DdF26, 155; MR45)

kite *n* [W&F, M] Letter secretly sent out of prison (prison use) (RHTB41, 257)

knot *n* Head (MR93)

lame *n* [M, R as "socially backward person"] Fool (probably from *lame brain*) (Labov [1972: passim] uses *lame* as 'outsider') (AL50; F3, 221; GDW126; J30, 33; H1; MR62, 72, 130, 176; PSM5, SL32)

lane *n* A variant, now commoner, of LAME (J30, 33; KM72)

last mile, the *n* corridor leading from cell block to execution chamber; inmate's trip to his execution, THE WING (usually with *take, walk*; prison use) (DR42)

lay for *vt* Wait for (DdF143)

lay [something] **down** *vt* [M] Explain, present in detail (WE12)

lay in the cut *vi* Wait secretly, remain hidden, lie low (DdF159)

lay two ways *v phr* Trick somebody by returning less than the proper amount of money, short-change (SL37)

lay up *vi* [M, C] Be idle (J35)

legal aid *n* Lawyer appointed for defense of indigent defendant (from Legal Aid Society); hence, any incompetent or indifferent defense lawyer (DR63)

lid *n* 1: [W&F, M, C, R] Hat, CROWN, SHY, SKY, STRAW (BSm11)   2: See HEAD (F105)

like stink on shit *adv* Immediately, at once (with verbs of motion) (2SM32)

long *adj* [M] Plentiful (of money) (AL58; F119, 147; GDW111); extreme, severe (of a narcotics habit) (DJ36; HTB91)

long-shoe game *n* Pimping (from narrow, pointed [RAT-DRAWN] shoe fashionable among pimps; often used as a synonym for THE LIFE) (BSm8; HTB108; MLSG title, 25) In MR the narrator takes his nickname from this game.)

luck out on *vt* Beat in competition through luck rather than skill (PSM50)

lug *n* [W&F] Demand (usually for money) (F214)

mack *n* 1: Skilled, clever operator (DdF39 [of a woman])   2: Trade of MACKMAN (MLSG5)   *vi* Operate as a MACKMAN (DYC22; WE14)

mackman *n* [W&F, C, as 'pimp'] Pimp, esp. one who controls and organizes every aspect of the life of the girls in his STABLE without soliciting for them (From French *maquereau* 'pimp, pander.' A very old word in English as *mackerel*, it is cited by Farmer and Henley [1970] as far back as Caxton, 1483.) (BSm1, 55; MLSG18; MR71, 178; PS69)

main girl *n* Principal prostitute in a STABLE, closest female to a pimp (AL53; RHTB44)

main man *n* [C, R] Closest male friend (DR31; GDW37; L31, 33, 40, 60, 62; RHTB245)

man *n* Close male friend (with possessive) (DdF3, 6; MR69)

man, the *n* [W&F, M, C, R] Person in authority, policeman, prison guard (GDW152; 2HK9; HTB64; L3; RHTB305; SL66)

mark *n* 1: [W&F, M] Victim of a crime, esp. of a confidence game; hence, stupid or gullible person (F76)   2: Letter: anything written or printed, SCRIBE, SCRIP, SCRIPT (RHTB201)

mellow *n* [C] Close friend (RHTB229)   *adj* [M, C] Excellent (F117)

[Miss/Mrs.] **Murphy walker** *n* One who engages in the MURPHY, a MURPHY-MAN (SL55)

mommy *n* A man's term of address to a lover (KB33)

motherfucker *n* Person (not necessarily pejorative) (BMD70; 80)

motherfucking *adj* An intensive (not necessarily pejorative) (BMD16, MR76, 97, 132, 139, 144; OTD20)

mud-kicker See KICK MUD

Murphy, the *n* The [Miss/Mrs.] Murphy game, a confidence trick in which a victim is directed to a fictitious prostitute but told he must first surrender his valuables to "[Miss/Mrs.] Murphy," the confidence man's accomplice, for safekeeping (MR124)

Murphy-man *n* See [Miss/Mrs.] MURPHY WALKER

my man *n* [M] In direct address, friendly epithet (DJ6; KB1; MR19; RHTB264)

narco n [W&F²] Detective on police narcotics squad; federal narcotics agent (GDW39; HTB107, 138; KB46 attrib; RHTB126, 283 attrib)

noble n Influential prison inmate (prison use) (RHTB14)

nod vi [W&F², M, C] Experience drowsiness as a result of narcotics (F95; KB27; KH48)

nut, on the See ON THE NUT

off vt [M, C, R] Kill, murder (RHTB283)

on the nut adj phr Without money (KM8)

on the roam adj phr Walking the street (of a prostitute) (L21)

pad n [W&F, M, C, R] Residence, CRIB, SHACK (AL38; F16; DdF27, 103, 121; GDW36; HTB32, 48; KB37; SH30)

papa n A term of address from a woman to her lover or pimp (DdF163; MR160)

paper-hang, the n [W&F] Act of forging or passing bad checks (SL37)

pedigree n Personal history, record, background (BD13; BMD60, 74; F8; DdF162; KB14; KM111)

peep vt [C] Look at, esp. something hidden (variant of *peek*) (L48; MR72; PS24)

piece n [W&F, M, C] Gun, esp. pistol (DR38)

pin vi, vt [W&F, M, C, R] Watch, look at, scrutinize, examine (DdF64; GDW73; HTB21, KB9; L28)

pink n [W&F, M] Caucasian (KM32)

play n Property, assets, proceeds (KM84; SH39)   vi, vt See HUSTLE (BSm73; DYC19; F4; DdF34, 104; HTB149; KM53, 104; L15; MR124; PS59; RHTB81; SL39)

player n See HUSTLER (DdF45; KM109)

P.O. n Parole officer (GDW152)

poke n [W&F] See HIDE; roll of money (F18)

pop vt 1: Penetrate sexually (AL19; BF36)   2: Shoot bullets (DR38)

pot n Vagina (Eric Partridge [1949] cites *pot* as 'a woman.') (AL25)

pound n [W&F] Five dollars (from pound sterling) (DJ11; MR15)

pressed adj [C] See CLEAN (DdF13, 21, 121; MR19)

prop n Proposition (MR98)

pros, pross n Prostitute (HTB97)

P-.38 n Thirty-eight caliber police revolver (H11)

pull vt 1: [W&F] Arrest (from pull in) (HTB77)   2: Recruit (prostitutes) (BSm20; DYC16; MLSG14; MR10, 27, 155; PS69; SH16)

pull off vt [W&F] Accomplish, succeed in (BL13; SH6)

push vt [W&F] Drive (a motor vehicle) (KB29)

pussy n Coward (from pussy 'vagina, woman') (DR88)

put [one's] **ass on** [one's] **shoulder** v phr Apply [oneself] diligently, get on the ball, put [one's] nose to the grindstone (DYC35)

put [someone] **down** vt [W&F, M] Defeat verbally, insult (PS39)

put (keep) [one's] **foot in** [someone's] **ass** v phr Abuse, beat (DYC36)

put [someone] **in the cross** See IN THE CROSS

put [someone] **on ice** vt [W&F] Kill (BSk30)

put [someone] **wise** vt Inform, clarify something for (put 'make' + wise 'aware') (KB2)

queen n [W&F, M] Beautiful woman, STALLION (DdF78; KB9, 35; MR87)

quiet as it's kept adv [M] Although it's not generally known (L69)

quilty adj Luxurious (of clothes) (DdF10)

rank vt Overestimate, overplay (a HAND) (F149)

rap vi [W&F, M, C, R] Talk, converse (possibly from prison usage, 'communicate during periods of enforced silence by tapping on walls') (DJ44; RHTB247)

rat-drawn adj Pointed (of shoes) (SLee3)

rod n Penis (F140)

roll vt Open (a prison cell) (prison use, always in roll 'em) (RHTB306)

roller n Policeman (from patroller, cited and glossed by Joel Chandler Harris [1862] (F245; GDW35; KB5; KM21)

romp vi Stamp (usually with stomp [from stamp], possibly from rampage; M defines romp as 'to dance to music') (SM33) vt Beat, stamp on (SM76)

round vi Turn around (GDW132)

round-eye n Anus; hence, anal sex, BOOTY (F121)

rub n See STING (DdF105)

run down vt [M, R] Relate, disclose (BMD60; SH15)

rush n Exhilaration from rush of blood as a first effect of taking narcotics (KH47)

scan on vt Examine (usually something to be stolen) (SL62)

scheme on [someone] vt Scheme to take advantage of (SL34)

scoil vi Scald + boil (PSM64)

score n [W&F] Something gained by trickery or luck (AL34) vi [W&F] See COP (HTB30, 40, 45)

screw n [W&F] Prison guard (from turnscrew 'man who turns screw [of obsolete locking device]') (RHTB177)

scribe n [W&F, M] See MARK (AL1; L4) vt [W&F] Write (RHTB41)

scrip n See MARK (RHTB47)

script n [W&F] See MARK (RHTB194)

see [someone] **straight** v phr Provide for, take care of (See STRAIGHT) (GDW70)

set n Scene of operations (BL8; GDW76; RHTB246)

shack n [C] See PAD (DdF159)

shade n [W&F] Negro (cited by W&F as derogatory from 1865) (KM32)

shag vi Engage in sexual intercourse (possibly from shag 'a fast dance') (DdF109)

shit n 1: Material, substance; things (not necessarily pejorative) (F99, 217; MR128; SH32)   2: [W&F] Narcotics, esp. heroin (DJ41; HTB53; WE39)

shit, not to be v phr Be worthless (whence the old joke "Someone said you ain't shit, but I stuck up for you. I said you were.") (AL14)

shoddy-doo n The act of slapping another's palm in greeting, SPLOW (RHTB234)

shoot vt [W&F] Inject (narcotics) (F150, 156, 160; DJ41)

short n [W&F, M, C, R] Car (probably from 'short way to travel') (AL35; DdF108; GDW23; L58, 75; RHTB286)   adj [W&F] Insufficient, deficient (of money) (BSm39; GDW115)

short heist n Criminal sexuality; hence, pornography (possibly from short 'small, mean' + heist 'stickup,' generalized to any crime; hence, 'low, unworthy crime') (DR46 attrib)

shortstop n Fool; insignificant person (MR176)

shot n Pickpocket (F73 attrib; SL61)

shuck, the n Fraud, trickery (HTB43)

shy n See LID (KM15)

sick adj [W&F, M] In need of narcotics; suffering from withdrawal of narcotics (HTB47)

signify vi [R] Make covert references, imply something, insinuate, cast indirect aspersions; goad or taunt by innuendo; arouse animosity between others by indirection. (W&F define signify as "to pretend to have knowledge; to pretend to be hip, especially when such pretensions cause one to trifle with an important matter"; but as Abrahams [1970:264] points out, its uses are much broader, including "boast by indirect or gestural means." Ralph Ellison [1964:6] defines signifying more tersely as "rhetorical understatement," and M limits the meaning to that form of ritualized insult-exchange called "playing the dozens," defining *signify* as "to censure in twelve or fewer statements." R is closer to the truth with "language behavior that makes direct or indirect implications of baiting [sic] or boasting, the essence of which is making fun of another's appearance, relatives, or situation." All of these definitions have in common the essential feature of insinuation or indirection. The Milners [1973:307] note only the hostile element of *signifying* in defining it as "to cause trouble, to instigate, to stir up, although often in fun." For the most comprehensive study of this term and its application, see Claudia Mitchell-Kernan [1971].) (DYC22; SM title, 2, 7, 40, 65, 80, 92

simp *vi* Be or act simple-minded (F92, 262)

skin *n* Crime, esp. confidence trick (HTB69)

sky *n* [W&F, M, R "sky piece"] See LID (GDW11)

slide 1: *n* [W&F, R] Pants pocket (originally pickpocket use, 'place into which to slide one's hand') (GDW84; KB23)   2: *vi* [W&F, C, R] Leave (F237)

sling, in a See IN A SLING

smack *n* [W&F, M, C] Heroin (from Yiddish shmeck 'smell') (DJ12; GDW33; HTB51, KB8)

snow *n* [W&F] Cocaine (from the color) (DdF72)

snuff *vt* [W&F²] Kill, murder (DJ46)

solids *n* Substantial help (with *do* 'render') (HTB34)

sound *vi* [R] Bluster, brag (MR74)

spike *n* [W&F², C, R] Hypodermic needle; anything used as a hypodermic needle (2HK24; HTB49; J36; WE17)

split *vt* Leave from (SH4)

splow *n* See SHODDY-DOO (RHTB234)

sporting life *n* The Life; the black, urban subculture that generates toasts (The character Sportin' Life in DuBose Heyward's *Porgy* [1925] takes his name from his participation in this community.) (SL title)

spread *n* Round of play in cards (BSk13; PSM63, 65) *vt* Play (cards) (BSk4, 10)

square john *n* [W&F] Man outside the Life, respectable man; dupe (WE27)

stable *n* [W&F, M, C] Group of prostitutes working for one pimp (F208; KB31)

stallion *n* [M, C, R] See QUEEN (A curious use, considering the usual associations of the word.) (MR87)

stash *n* [W&F] Hiding place; things hidden (KB16) —**stashed** *adj* provided, supplied, having reserves (2SM23)

stick *n* [C] Specialty, special talent or preference (from Yiddish *shtik* 'bit, piece, special piece of stage business') (DdF34; MR105)

sting *n* Accomplishment or instance of a crime, esp. a confidence trick, RUB, GIG (widely known since the movie *The Sting* [1973]) (BL13; DdF115; HTB42; SH6)

stomp-down *adj* Complete, dedicated, hard-working (of a prostitute) (BMD18; DR32; PS9)

stone *adj* [R] Complete, unreserved, real, COLD-BLOODED, TURNED OUT (An intensive probably taken from its adverbial use with literal meaning in expressions like stone dead, stone cold, stone blind; the usage is noted by Abrahams [1970:264].) (DR88; KB15; MR76)

stone-cold *adj* See STONE, of which it is an elaborated form with no added meaning (MR76)

straight *adj* Provided, satisfactorily situated. See SEE STRAIGHT (GDW70)

straighten *vt* Repay, settle accounts with (GDW163)

straw *n* See LID (PS36)

stud *n* [W&F, M, C, R] Male person (with no connotations of virility) (HTB1, 21, 25, 57, 59, 75: MLSG15; MR70)

stuff *n* 1: [W&F] Narcotics, esp. heroin (DR30; F95; GDW67; HTB36; KB38; MR123; RHTB268; SL71)   2: See THE SHUCK (F75; KB4; SL39) —**play stuff** *v phr* Engage in a confidence game, trick someone, decieve (F75; KB4; SL39)

swag [W&F, M] Money or goods (usually illicitly obtained) (F225)

sweet-loving *adj* Adept at sexual performance (of a prostitute) (GDW122; PS40 [nickname])

swipe *n* Penis (black use) (BF70)

take [someone] **off** *vt* [W&F, M] Trick, rob (DdF145; WE22)

take the weight *v phr* Accept the punishment, serve the prison sentence (MR126)

tall *adj* See LONG (of a narcotics habit) (F179)

tap *vt* Inject (needle) (WE17)

tea *n* [W&F] Marijuana (WE36)

the way . . . *conj* Which is why . . . . (BSk6)

thoroughbred *n* Superior or dependable person, expert (F226; DdF114; KM112, 138; L38; MR69, 145; RHTB254)

threads *n pl* [W&F, M, C, R] Men's clothes, esp. a suit (AL27; BSm12; F159; RHTB249)

three *n* Three-dollar BAG of heroin (see 2KH6) (KB23)

throw *vt* Overcome; hence arrest (HTB81)

tip *vi* Notice, discover (something) (DdF47)

toast *n* [R lists *toast* as an adjective 'good, fine, acceptable'] Folk poem of the Life (BSk6; KB48; 2KH31; MR169; RHTB324)

tough *adj* [W&F, M, C, R] See BAD (MR20; RHTB175, 266)   *adv* Much, well (F95)

tracks *n pl* [W&F, C] Marks or scars from hypodermic injection of narcotics (a reference to both their appearance and their being taken by the police as an indication of narcotics use) (F95)

trick *n* [W&F, M] Prostitute's customer (See Dundes [1973: 332n] for extended discussion of this term.) (BMD7; F72, 84, 131, 143; DdF122; GDW82, 89, 93; KB16; KM48, 60; L70; MLSG19; MR64, 65, 76; PS33; SM14; SL7, 54)   *vi* Engage in sexual activity for money (F127, 133, 135, 137, 138)

trick house *n* House of prostitution (F229)

turn *vt* [C] Serve (a customer) sexually (with TRICK) (BSm22, 54; F89; MR130; SM14; SL54)

turned out *adj* An intensive (see COLD-BLOODED, STONE, STOMP-DOWN) (KB15)

unravel *vt* Disclose, tell (F8)

untie *vi* Remove band (usually belt) placed on arm to make vein stand out for injection (HBT57)

unwind *vt* Unfold, tell (DdF61)

upside *prep* [R lists *upside one's head*] Alongside, up against (KB41; L61)

up tight *adj* 1: [C, R] In trouble, under control of another (L44; RHTB53, 215)   2: [M] Satisfied, elevated, in a narcotic state (2KH16, L36)   3: [C] Intimate, emotionally involved (DdF130; GDW76, 117; L59)

vice *vt* Take advantage of, put pressure on (SL36)

vine *n* [W&F, M, C, R] Clothes, esp. man's suit (BSm10; DJ5; GDW119, 142; HTB15, 94, 105; MR13, 21; RHTB247) See THREADS

viper *n* [W&F, M as 'drug dealer'] Marijuana addict (SL51)

waste *vt* [W&F] Beat severely, destroy; [M] Kill (KB42)

wheel *vi* Turn (GDW 93)

white-on-white *n* White-on-white shirt of a fabric stylish in the 1940's (GDW29; HTB5)

wife-in-law *n* Prostitute subordinate to principal woman in a STABLE ("If you're working for a pimp who isn't married to you, the girls you work with are your sisters-in-law. But if the pimp is your husband, then the girls are called 'wife-in-law.' "—Florrie Fisher [1971:80].) (F184)

wig *vt* [W&F] Startle; delight (DdF129)

Wing, the See LAST MILE (DR15)

wire *n* [W&F] News, report, information (RHTB288; SM25)

zanzy *adj* [M] See FOXY (SH12)

Bibliography
of Works Consulted

The following titles are listed alphabetically by author. Where two or more entries by the same author are included, they are given chronologically.

Abrahams, Roger D. "The Toast: A Neglected Form of Folk Narrative." In *Folklore in Action*, ed. Horace P. Beck. Philadelphia: American Folklore Society, 1962A. Pp. 1–11. A summary essay on the subject, largely repeated in *Deep Down in the Jungle*. Superficial but a good introduction, illustrated with three examples.

———. "Playing the Dozens." *Journal of American Folklore*, 75 (1962B), 209–220. A psychological interpretation of the ritual contest, this article contains some questionable theorizing but many useful examples. Among the best criticisms of Abrahams' explanations is Dundes' introduction to the article in his *Mother Wit* (1973:295–297), q.v.

———. *Positively Black*. Englewood Cliffs, N.J.: Prentice-Hall, 1970A. An informed examination of urban black culture using much toast material for illustration.

———. "The Negro Stereotype: Negro Folklore and the Riots." *Journal of American Folklore*, 83 (1970B), 229–258. Some of the ideas Abrahams has developed elsewhere are applied here to the racial conflicts of the late 1960's.

———. *Deep Down in the Jungle: Negro Narrative Folklore from the*

193

Streets of Philadelphia. 2d ed.; Chicago: Aldine, 1970C. The pioneer study of toasts, Abrahams' book contains many, and it attempts to relate them to their social and ethnic matrix. Restricted source area somewhat limits the utility of this work, but the volume has many striking and suggestive observations and much valuable material.

Agar, Michael H. "Folklore of the Heroin Addict: Two Examples." *Journal of American Folklore*, 84 (1971), 175–185. Interesting examination of "Honky-Tonk Bud" and "King Heroin," collected from addicts at the Lexington, Ky., Clinical Research Center for narcotics addicts. Deals with material as literature of the narcotics addict culture.

————. *Ripping and Running: A Formal Ethnography of Urban Heroin Addicts*. New York: Seminar Press (Harcourt Brace Jovanovich), 1973. A perceptive study of addict life as a subculture of urban American society by a noted cultural anthropologist. A highly professional treatment, systematically presented and developed.

Bark, James. "Pornography and Bawdry in Literature and Society." In *The Merry Muses of Caledonia*. Ed. J. Bark, and Sidney Goodsir Smith. New York: Gramercy, 1959. Informative essay accompanying classic Robert Burns collection of bawdy Scottish ballads first published in 1799.

Beck, Robert (as Iceberg Slim). *Pimp: The Story of My Life*. Los Angeles: Holloway House, 1969A. Autobiography of a black pimp. An extraordinary inside view of the Life told without bitterness or moralizing.

————. *Mama Black Widow*. Los Angeles: Holloway House, 1969B. Biography of a black homosexual. Like Beck's other books a vivid picture of ghetto life.

————. *Trick Baby: The Story of a White Negro*. Los Angeles: Holloway House, 1969C. Biography of a light-skinned con man in the Chicago black ghetto. An interesting account of confidence hustles.

————. *The Naked Soul of Iceberg Slim*. Los Angeles: Holloway House, 1971. A collection of essays on life in the ghetto by a perceptive and sensitive insider.

Binderman, Murray B, Dennis Wepman, and Ronald B. Newman. "A Portrait of 'the Life.' " *Urban Life*, 4 (1975), 213–225. An exploration of urban black experience as reflected in toasts.

Brearley, H.C. " 'Ba-ad Nigger.' " *South Atlantic Quarterly*, 38 (1939), pp. 75–81. Wide-ranging study of black use of "bad" with favorable significance.

Brown, H. Rap. *Die, Nigger, Die!* New York: Dial Press, 1969. Polemic with much valuable information on life in the ghetto.

Brown, Stirling Allen. *Negro Poetry and Drama*, Bronze Booklet No. 7; Washington, D.C.: Associates in Negro Folk Education, 1937. Dated, but for its time and earlier an ample survey written with scholarship and rare perception. An excellent survey of both folk and literary material.

Buehler, Richard E. "Stacker Lee: A Partial Investigation into the Historicity of the Negro Murder Ballad." *Keystone Folklore Quarterly*, 12 (1967), 187–191. Interesting summary of information on the sources of the toast.

Claerbut, David. *Black Jargon in White America.* Grand Rapids, Mich.: William B. Eerdmans, 1972. Essentially a study of black-white communication, this little volume, based on a master's thesis, contains 45 pages of chatty preface to 30 pages of glossary. Unsophisticated and unreliable.

Clark, Kenneth. *Dark Ghetto.* New York: Harper & Row, 1965. An insightful survey of the black ghetto.

Dillard, John Lee. *Black English: Its History and Usage in the U.S.* New York: Random House, 1972. The first extended popular analysis of United States black English dialect. Marred by tendentious sociological and pedagogical views, but a generally dependable and useful examination of its subject.

Dollard, John. "The Dozens: Dialect of Insult." *American Imago*, 1 (1939), 3–25. The classic study of this curious form of verbal play; now somewhat dated but still the cornerstone of the literature on the subject.

Dorson, Richard M. *American Negro Folktales.* New York: Fawcett, 1967. An excellent popular survey by a leading folklorist.

Drake, St. Clair, and Horace Cayton. *Black Metropolis.* New York: Harper & Row, 1945. A now somewhat dated but generally reliable study of the black urban lower class, showing it in all its diversity.

Dundes, Alan (ed.). *Mother Wit from the Laughing Barrel: Readings in the Interpretation of Afro-American Folklore.* Englewood Cliffs, N.J.: Prentice-Hall, 1973. Outstanding anthology of material on all aspects of United States black culture, superbly edited by a leading folklorist.

Eddington, Neil Arthur. "The Urban Plantation: The Ethnography of an Oral Tradition in a Negro Community." Ph. D. dissertation, University of California at Berkeley, 1967. Folkloristic study of a black San Francisco community, examines the interrelationships between society and language behavior. Taped conversations are transcribed and analyzed at length, and a specimen toast is presented. Dr. Eddington makes a cogent argument for the value to social theorists of material from oral tradition. Good, brief glossary.

Ellison, Ralph. "The Blues." Review of *Blues People* by LeRoi Jones, in *New York Review of Books,* Feb. 6, 1964, pp. 5–7. Sharply critical of Jones' "theory of American Negro culture [which] can only contribute more confusion than clarity."

Farmer, J. S., and W. E. Henley. *Slang and Its Analogues.* Rev. ed.; New York: Arno Press, 1970. A classic text, originally published in 7 volumes from 1890 to 1904. Immense scholarship in obsolete slang and folk speech, supported by quotations going back four centuries, make this the basic book in its field.

Fiddle, Seymour. *Portraits from a Shooting Gallery: Life Styles from the Drug Addict World.* New York: Harper & Row, 1967. A penetrating look at the culture of narcotics addiction drawn from taped conversations with addicts at New York's Exodus House. Sociologist Fiddle presents three such conversations *in extenso* with incisive comments.

———. *New York Addict Argot New and Old.* New York: Exodus House, 1972A. An unprofessional but useful glossary of expressions heard among the addicts at Exodus House. Contains some terms found in toasts and uncited elsewhere.

———. *Toasts: Images of a Victim Society.* New York: Exodus House, 1972B. Gives thirteen toasts and discusses them, in an original and somewhat slanted introduction, as "concerning drug users and drug experiences."

Fisher, Florrie. *The Lonely Trip Back.* New York: Doubleday, 1971. An honest and often moving account of the author's life as an addict.

Hall, Susan, and Bob Adelman. *Gentleman of Leisure.* New York: New American Library, 1973. A study of a successful black pimp by a photojournalist team, this volume catches with camera and tape-recorder the flamboyant style of the Life.

Harris, Joel Chandler. *Uncle Remus, His Songs and Ballads.* New York, Houghton Mifflin, 1862. Dialect verses effectively capturing and sometimes glossing folk speech of plantation blacks.

Heyward, DuBose. *Porgy.* New York: George H. Doran, 1925. Touching novel set in South Carolina. The character Sportin' Life from New Orleans is an effective early depiction of the hustler in literature.

Hughes, Langston, and Arna Bontemps. *The Book of Negro Folklore.* New York: Dodd, Mead, 1958. Entertaining volume; contains a few toasts not identified as such.

Hurston, Zora Neale. "Story in Harlem Slang." *American Mercury,* 45 (1942), 84–96. A useful little glossary of Harlem street talk effectively illustrated in dialogue.

Iceberg Slim. *See* Robert Beck.

Jackson, Bruce. "Prison Folklore." *Journal of American Folklore,* 78 (1965A), 317–329. Very astute study of prisoner subculture; discusses and cites some toasts.

———. "Stagolee Stories: A Badman Goes Gentle." *Southern Folklore Quarterly,* 29 (1965B), 228–233. Solid research into the history of one of the best-known toast stories.

———. "Circus and Street: Psychosocial aspects of the Black Toast." *Journal of American Folklore,* 85 (1972A) 123–139. Draws a strained and somewhat fanciful analogy, but contains six toasts and some provocative ideas.

———. *In the Life: Versions of the Criminal Experience.* New York: Holt, Rinehart & Winston, 1972B. "A tour of the underworld by the people who live there." Quoting a number of hustlers, provides a striking view of the Life from the inside.

———. "The 'Titanic' Toast." In *Veins of Humor,* ed. Harry Levin. Harvard English Studies No. 3, Cambridge, Mass.: Harvard University Press, 1972C. An extended study of a classic toast.

———. *"Get Your Ass in the Water and Swim Like Me": Narrative Poetry from the Black Oral Tradition.* Cambridge, Mass.: Harvard University Press, 1974. The first really scientific collection of toasts, Jackson's book includes many poems which do not fall within the definition employed here. Impeccable scholarship and lively style.

Jones, LeRoi. *Blues People.* New York: Morrow, 1963. A highly contentious study of contemporary black life through its music by one of its more ardent polemicists.

———. *Black Music.* London: Macgibbon & Kee, 1969. Like *Blues People,* vigorous and feisty. Both should be used with caution.

Keil, Charles. *Urban Blues.* Chicago: University of Chicago Press, 1966. Deals with the blues singer as a culture hero, and analyzes the ghetto values reflected in the blues. A stimulating and illuminating book.

Kochman, Thomas (ed.). *Rappin' and Stylin' Out: Communications in Urban Black America.* Urbana, Ill.: University of Illinois

Press, 1972. A rich collection of articles on life and language in the black ghetto. Many references to toasts.

Labov, William, Paul Cohen, Clarence Robins, and John Lewis. "The Use of Language in the Speech Community." In *A Study of the Non-Standard English of Negro and Puerto Rican Speakers in New York*. Cooperative Research Project No. 3288, 2 vols; New York: Columbia University Press, 1968. Vol. II, pp. 55–75. A highly sophisticated study of toasts as both social behavior and folk artifact. Quotes several in whole or in part.

Liebow, Elliot. *Tally's Corner: a Study of Negro Streetcorner Men*. Boston: Little Brown, 1967. Effective, sometimes moving observation of black ghetto life in Washington, D.C.

Lightnin' Rod. *Hustlers Convention*. New York: Harmony Books (Crown), 1973. A narrative poem of over 1,000 lines written on the model of a toast. A credible fabrication until the end, where it assumes an improbable moralistic tone.

Lingeman, Richard R. *Drugs from A to Z: A Dictionary*. New York: McGraw-Hill, 1969. More pharmacology than sociolinguistics, this book nevertheless has some valuable and up-to-date material on the narcotics scene.

Lomax, John, and Alan Lomax. *American Ballads and Folk Songs*. New York: Macmillan, 1934. A wide-ranging collection which contains much of interest to the student of black folk material.

Lomax, Alan. "Folk Song Style." *American Anthropologist*, 61 (1959), 927–953. Overly generalized but provocative examination of the psychological substructure of folk music and poetry.

———. "Song Structure and Social Structure." *Ethnography*, 1 (1962), 425–453. Like "Folk Song Style," rather superficial but makes some useful observations.

Major, Clarence. *Dictionary of Afro-American Slang*. New York: International Publishers, 1970. An ambitious effort with dates for many of its entries but no citations to back them up. Linguistically so naive as to be almost unusable.

Maurer, David W., and Victor H. Vogel. *Narcotics and Narcotics Addiction*. 3d ed. Springfield, Ill.: Charles C Thomas, 1971. Originally published in 1954, this classic study of the narcotics problem is more legal and medical than cultural in orientation and is now quite dated; but Professor Maurer's 80-page glossary, "The Argot of the Narcotics Addict," remains definitive.

Melnick, Mimi Clar. " 'I Can Peep Through Muddy Water and Spy Dry Land': Boasts in the Blues." In *Folklore International: Essays in Traditional Literature. Belief, and Custom in Honor of Wayland Debs Hand*, ed. O. K. Wilgus. Hatboro, Pa.: Folklore Associates, 1967. Demonstrates some interesting parallels between toasts and blues.

Milner, Christina, and Richard Milner. *Black Players: The Secret World of Black Pimps*. Boston: Little Brown, 1973. An inside account by two anthropologists of the world's second oldest profession and, through it, of the Life. Contains a brief but useful glossary of "black hustling slang."

Mitchell-Kernan, Claudia. *Language Behavior in a Black Urban Community*. Monographs of the Language-Behavior Laboratory No. 2; Berkeley: University of California Press, 1971. An invaluable contribution to the literature on black speech by a black anthropological linguist with a fine ear for nuance.

Odum, Howard W., and Guy B. Johnson. *The Negro and His Songs*. Chapel Hill: University of North Carolina Press, 1925. An important early study of black folk music with wide implications for the study of toasts.

Partridge, Eric. *A Dictionary of the Underworld, British and American*. London: Macmillan, 1949. Perhaps the most scholarly treatment of its subject, though somewhat unreliable in its treatment of modern usage.

Radin, Paul. *The Trickster*. New York: Philosophical Library, 1956. The classic study of this archetypal figure in mythology and folklore.

Rainwater, Lee (ed.). *Soul*. Chicago: Aldine, 1970. A valuable collection of material on many aspects of black urban culture.

Reynolds, Anthony M. "Urban Negro Toasts: A Hustler's View from L.A." *Western Folklore*, 33 (1974), 267–300. Emphasizes the relation of hobo and cowboy lore to toast material, of which a fair sampling is quoted. Some good bibliographical and discographical material in the footnotes enhances a generally well-reasoned article which demonstrates by the California provenance of its texts the breadth of dispersion of toasts.

Roberts, Hermese E. *The Third Ear: A Black Glossary*. Chicago: English-Language Institute of America, 1971. A curious little entry in the lists of black lexicography, this 12-page pamphlet is too amateurish to be taken seriously as scholarship but contains some striking entries otherwise unavailable.

Rohrer, John H., and Munro S. Edmonson (eds.). *The Eighth Genera-*

tion Grows Up. New York: Harper & Row, 1960. A very illuminating examination of black ghetto life.

Wentworth, Harold, and Stuart Berg Flexner. *Dictionary of American Slang.* 2d ed.; New York: Thomas Y. Crowell, 1967. The
unchallenged leader in the field, a work of impressive scholarship and scrupulous rigor.

Wepman, Dennis, Ronald B. Newman, and Murray B. Binderman.
"Toasts: The Black Urban Folk Poetry." *Journal of American
Folklore,* 87 (1974), 208–224. A literary and sociological sur-
vey of toasts, relating them to the Life.

West, Hollie I. "The Confessions of Iceberg Slim." *Miami* (Florida)
Herald, May 20, 1973, *Tropic Magazine,* pp. 38–41. An
examination of recent changes in the character of the Life. An
interview with Robert Beck ("Iceberg Slim").

Index

Index of Titles
and First Lines